CHILDREN OF THE FUTURE

Frances Morrell

THE HOGARTH PRESS

LONDON

For my parents
Beatrice and Frank Galleway, now dead,
and for my brother Peter

Published in 1989 by
The Hogarth Press
30 Bedford Square, London WC1B 3SG

Copyright © Frances Morrell 1989

A CIP catalogue record for this book is available from the British Library

ISBN 0 7012 0819 8

Photoset by Rowland Phototypesetting Limited
Bury St Edmunds, Suffolk
Printed in Finland by
Werner Söderström Oy

Contents

Acknowledgements

A number of people have been generous enough to share the fruits of their scholarship and experience with me. I am greatly indebted to them.

Laurie South MA, Member of the Society of Education Officers was research adviser to the book. I am greatly indebted to him.

Sections of the book were read by Professor Harvey Goldstein of the Institute of Education; Dr Lewis Minkin of Manchester University; Terry Ward, the Cambridge economist; Alison Kelly; Alyson Price of Haverstock Comprehensive School; Christine Holloway; Professor Meghnad Desai of LSE; Harriet Bretherton; Andy Harris of Avon Education Department; Judith Cook; Charlotte Gibbons; Denis Felsenstein, formerly ILEA Schools Inspector; Colin Yardley, Head of Thomas Tallis Comprehensive School; Gail Wilson of LSE; Andrew Dilnot from the Institute for Fiscal Studies; Professor Ted Wragg of Exeter University kindly advised me on one section, Betty Hill on another. A number of people read the text whose positions make it inappropriate for me to name them. I would like to thank them just the same. Geraldine Constable typed the first draft – a labour of love.

I wish to record my appreciation for the help given by my editor, Jenny Uglow, herself a distinguished writer, and by the copy editor, the saintly Robert Lacey.

Robert Skidelsky encouraged me to write this book and I am grateful to him. He is especially absolved from responsibility for the final outcome since he has not seen it.

Finally, my thanks to my daughter Daisy and husband Brian Morrell for their patience with the author at the other end of the kitchen table.

Introduction

In January 1988 I interviewed a most lucid European politician, Michel Rocard. Today he is a somewhat embattled Prime Minister of France. We met at the Palais de Congrès in Paris, where the French Socialist Party had gathered for a final conference before the French Presidential Elections, scheduled for May.

Democratic politicians are usually at their most hardheaded when standing in the shadow of the ballot box, so it was with particular interest that I asked M. Rocard what, in his opinion, was the single most important issue the French people should consider as they went to the polls. 'Education,' he replied immediately. 'In terms of dignity, in terms of social ethics, economic efficiency and the struggle against unemployment, education happens to be the key.'

In my experience such a response is unusual. Top public figures here are drawn to the more macho Ministries – Defence, Industry, the Treasury – and their personal preferences shape their policy analysis. Yet Michel Rocard's priorities were shared both by his colleagues and by his rivals in the other political parties. The French elections in 1988 were dominated by concern about 1992, the date when a single European market, a Europe without frontiers, comes into being. Ambitious industrialists were looking forward to expanding into Great Britain and other EEC countries. At the same time they were worried that European competitors might expand into France, causing the closure of weaker French enterprises and increasing unemployment.

To French political leaders the answer was obvious: public spending on education and training had to be increased to reduce unemployment, to help integrate the minority communities, to remedy the shortage of workers skilled in high-tech areas and generally to help France to prepare for 1992 and for the further threat, still below the economic horizon, of the Pacific rim economies of the East. Today that programme is being implemented.

Listening to M. Rocard, I found it extraordinary to reflect that, although 1992 posed exactly the same problems for Britain, the issue had scarcely surfaced in the General Election of 1987. British companies too would be challenged on their home ground by European competitors. The fall in the number of people leaving school each year, combined with the need for high-tech expansion, is creating a skills shortage here as well, while at the same time unemployed people, concentrated in the North, in the inner cities and among the black communities, are experiencing poverty in the midst of plenty.

Managements, even in our top companies, are markedly less well educated and trained than their European counterparts: culturally we are unresponsive to the needs of manufacturing industry and the drive to export. Most of us do not even speak a single foreign language.

Yet while countries like France have concentrated on planning for their own economic survival, we in Britain have set aside such pragmatic ends – our 'reforms' issue from a philosophical perspective. Our Prime Minister and her intellectual advisers and supporters have criticised State planning *on principle* as a way of creating prosperity and providing hospitals, homes and schools. They have set out to alter the administration of the country either by placing more areas of responsibility in private hands, or by making publicly administered sectors operate according to market principles. By 1987 they were ready to apply these principles to the education service.

Spending on education as a whole has been reduced. The institutions which planned our school system are being deprived of their powers: the taxes which funded them are to be discontinued and the legal framework which enclosed them has been replaced. Schools are to compete with each other for custom and will stand or fall by their success in that struggle. And the whole change has been carried through at a speed so breathtaking that most people have scarcely had time to understand Mr Baker's plans, much less decide whether they agree with them.

It may well be that the drastic and sudden change in our pattern of education will in fact enable us to meet our economic needs, while the planned, publicly funded response of the French Government will fail. But it is more likely that Kenneth Baker, rushing through these changes, may have sowed the wind, in the old phrase, for his successors to reap the whirlwind. Suppose individual parents realise the disadvantageous consequences of his policies for their children at the same time as the inability of the schools to meet the commercial and industrial needs of the country at a vulnerable time becomes apparent. There will then be pressure to modify Mr Baker's system, either in law or in practice. We will face a crisis, unable to return to the old system because it has been destroyed, equally unable to envisage an alternative way forward.

The purpose of this book is to challenge the validity of the Government's approach to public education, and to propose an alternative. Its context is the collapse of confidence in the post-war egalitarian philosophy of education since the watershed year of 1976.

I wish to argue that, side by side with the economic crises of the late 1970s which halted the expansion of public services, a management crisis was developing in education.

The roots of that crisis lay in the deficiencies of the 1944 Education Act, but they also reached back beyond that into long-standing British educational traditions.

The inability of the egalitarian generation of political leaders and thinkers to resolve that crisis, revise their goals and alter their strategy accordingly created a vacuum in educational policy. It was filled by a reactionary ethic and plan which today provides the framework and content of our school system. But the defeat of the egalitarian dream was *not* inevitable. It arose out of a failure to face, intellectually and practically, what equality really means from the point of view of each child.

How good was the record of the egalitarian generation? How accurate were the claims of their reactionary critics, who campaigned so effectively against them? What will be the consequences for our children of the 1988 Education Act? And is there another path which could have been chosen – and which we could still choose, even now? These are the questions which I have asked, and have attempted to answer as dispassionately as I can. This book is written as a contribution to the continuing debate which is taking place in Parliament, in the national media and educational journals, in council chambers, school governing bodies and staffrooms throughout the country. It is also written for parents, teachers, governors, lunch supervisors, students, lecturers – all those who, when the television lights have been switched off and the political cavalcade has moved on, will be left amongst the rubble, picking up the pieces and rebuilding the education service according to the new dispensation. It is an attempt to record the successes and failures of the old system; to look as fairly as possible at the strengths and weaknesses of the new plan and to consider what we should do next. And of course it is written on behalf of our children, not just those in the schools now, but the children of the future.

I should say at once that I believe our education service should be planned and paid for out of taxes: schools cannot be run like so many stalls in a market. But experience has also taught me that post-war planning *was* in need of reform.

In 1974 I signed the Official Secrets Act and entered the closed world of Whitehall, first as an adviser in the Department of Industry and afterwards in the Department of Energy. There, in the pre-Thatcher era, mandarins from the Treasury and the industrial Departments of State sat down with managers from the great fuel corporations and barons of the private sector to plan the supply of coal, steel, gas, oil and nuclear energy for the whole economy. As a result of these endeavours, investment was maintained in the energy industries although it dropped in the private manufacturing sector. But the conditions of secrecy within which the process was contained led to something like corruption. I do not believe, for example, that we will ever know what the true cost of the post-war nuclear programme has been: the figures could never be uncovered and pieced together by the most determined archivist, even if they were allowed to search the files.

'What does this constitutional nicety matter?' you may ask. It matters a great deal. The Department of Energy is under a statutory responsibility to provide energy at the lowest possible cost consistent with security of supply. The House of Commons is supposed to hold the Minister to account for the performance of those duties. Lacking information about the nuclear programme, MPs over the years have simply not been able to tell whether the Secretary of State was doing his duty – and that makes a nonsense of Parliament and democracy. It also means that families may have paid unnecessarily high electricity bills for a quarter of a century.

For six years, from 1981, I was at the head of the Inner London Education Authority, a body as large as a Government Department which planned the education service for the whole of London. Here again the planning process was indefensibly secret. As I pointed out to senior officials soon after I arrived, not one piece of information that would enable parents to make informed judgements about the relative performances of London schools was published: examination results by named schools, cross-indexed with the numbers and bands of pupils and the number of teachers per school were not disclosed. It took me years to persuade my colleagues to adopt an open publications policy. The first time I proposed it I was defeated in public committee by my own side. Most other local education authorities did not even collect the information needed to enable them to judge the relative quality of schools. They planned in self-imposed ignorance.

The suppression of information about the nuclear programme suited public officials and private sector companies: the lack of information about the quality of schooling in London and elsewhere suited officials and some leaders of the teaching unions. Politicians of all parties went along with different aspects of this system, which hid the truth from the consumer and the voter. I opposed the corporate conspiracy while in government and at ILEA. I will not defend it now.

The Thatcherite criticism of public planning has not been entirely misplaced: the record of those who ran the education service is not free from error. I myself made mistakes and learned from them. It is in this spirit that I examine the record with the humility appropriate to hindsight.

Although I accept that the planning of public services in the post-war period developed defects, I still believe it to be possible to plan an education service which offers equality of opportunity. By this I mean that every child, irrespective of gender, ethnic origin, social class or geography of birth should have access to equally good facilities, free and in their own locality, to help them express their own abilities and aptitudes to the full. I also believe that *only* by public planning can this be achieved.

*

In considering these complex matters, two scenes from my girlhood have often come back to me, two frozen moments as clear as a couple of stills from a fifties film on display outside a cinema.

In the first I am standing beside the utility table in the small and smoky living room of a terraced house in Yorkshire. It is mid-evening and my father, still in his work clothes, is looking at a textbook which appeared to be composed largely of complicated technical diagrams. I knew that it was his ambition to get 'on the staff' of his company, to become monthly paid and to lose the permanent fear of being given a week's notice.

I asked him if he was studying in order to gain promotion. 'It's too late,' he replied. I knew what he meant. At that time he was working in the neighbouring town of Leeds – we lived in York – and got up each day at 5 o'clock in the morning to travel there by bus, returning at 7 o'clock at night with time just to eat his supper, sit exhausted by the fire for half an hour, lay out his breakfast and go to bed. Such an environment would probably have defeated Einstein. Both he and my mother, who worked in Rowntree's factory packing chocolates, keenly felt their lack of education. At their wish I went to the local grammar school, though my mother warned me: 'That school is trying to make you ashamed of us.'

The second scene takes place in Rowntree's factory itself, where a group of girls from the grammar school, including me, were being shown around by management on an educational visit after O-levels.

Our guide paused beside a young woman who was packing chocolates into boxes at incredible speed but who was not introduced to us as the manager continued his dissertation. She was wearing a white turban and overalls: I was dressed in my school uniform of navy blazer with its badge and Latin motto, ugly brown lace-up shoes and unbecoming beret. We recognised each other at once, though we had not met since we were 11 years old: we had shared a desk at junior school. She did not speak to me. I did not know how to speak to her.

What is the significance of these scenes to me and the purpose of recounting them? The education system people advocate reflects the kind of society they desire, for the one naturally leads to the other. My parents' experience and my mother's words remind me why I believe so strongly in an education service in which every child has an equal chance and is treated with equal respect. That is why I believe in comprehensive education. People often say that we should keep politics out of education. I understand that sentiment and sympathise with it, but the choice of an education system and therefore of the desired society has to be made, and for my part I wish to be recorded openly as being on the side of equality. Some people will tell me that society has changed, that the old working class amongst which I grew up has disappeared, and that the case for equality is simply no longer relevant, an anachronism. I accept that change has taken place, much of it desirable. Our society is wealthier and many people's life chances have expanded accordingly. But the overwhelming majority of families still cannot possibly afford to pay for a private sector education for their children. Most cannot even afford the fees for 'extras' and the voluntary contributions that are increasingly being required in State schools, much less the full cost of higher education.

Most people, whether they have children or not, would, I believe, prefer to pay a level of tax that would ensure that every child receives a first-class education, free and near home. Some would do this solely on ethical grounds, but most would understand that the skills of our people are the chief asset of our society. Developing these skills is our best investment, and it is education which provides the means.

ONE

The Counter Revolutionaries

Philosophy is one of the few subjects which has not yet been proposed as a foundation element of the national curriculum to be studied by every child until the age of 16. In some ways this is a pity. Our national tradition, which is pragmatic, empirical and anti-intellectual, has its advantages, but enabling us to understand what is happening in public life today is not one of them.

The Education Reform Act of 1988 alters the organisation of State schooling in England and Wales from a national service planned and administered on an area basis in partnership with elected local authorities to what is, in effect, a market system. Secondary and large primary schools are to be self-governing. A body composed of parent representatives, teacher representatives and nominees from the local education authority and local business will organise the budget, hire staff, run the affairs of the school and compete for parental custom against other schools.

Each school is required to 'sell' the same goods, in the form of a standard national curriculum which will be subject to a standard testing system. Parallel changes in the financing arrangements involve a reduced Government contribution and the replacement of the local rate with a standard tax on business to be collected and distributed by Government and a flat rate tax on each adult, to be levied by the local council.

This huge alteration in the organisation of our schools has been discussed in the media as if it resulted from an analysis of research on how best to teach children. Yet the education system has in fact been dismantled and re-arranged according to an intellectual blueprint for the organisation of society, a blueprint whose first concern is not with education at all. Parents usually think that what happens in their local primary school must be independent of theories of the State. School governors, head teachers and local authority leaders may have the illusion that, within limits, they are managing and directing their own institutions. In fact, as John Maynard Keynes said in his *General Theory*: 'The ideas of economists and political philosophers, both when they are right and when they are wrong are more powerful than is commonly understood. Indeed, the world is ruled by little else. Practical men, who believe themselves to be quite exempt from any intellectual influences, are usually the slaves of some defunct econ-omist. Madmen in authority, who hear voices in the air are distilling their frenzy from some academic scribbler of a few years back.'[1]

The Education Reform Act may appear to be Mr Baker's child, but he is not in fact the father. If we wish to know why that Act was passed, what it is intended to achieve and to consider whether we support it, we will need to look first at the work of a group of intellectuals and only secondly at the evidence of the performance of the edu-cation service itself.

Who, then, are the writers who have, in some cases almost as a by-product of their work, created this huge upheaval in our schools and colleges? They are in the first place those thinkers who influenced Mrs Thatcher and other members of the present Government when they were in opposition during 1974–79 and who have provided the analysis and framework for the whole of this Govern-ment's policy during its subsequent ten years of office.

The most distinguished of these figures is undoubtedly Professor F. A. Hayek. Born in Vienna at the end of the last century, he is Chairman of the Adam Smith Institute,

Fellow of the London School of Economics, recipient of countless academic honours and author of a number of books restating the case for economic liberalism. One of his best-known books, *The Road to Serfdom*,[2] was written in London during the Second World War; ironically it was published in 1944, the year of the Education Act which set up the system which his philosophical ideas, forty years later, were to help to destroy.

Hayek is particularly concerned to argue against the involvement of Government in the life of the citizen. As he sees it, it is not the duty of Government to seek to implement some utopian vision by ensuring social justice, supporting equality or encouraging arrangements that will theoretically produce human happiness. Government's job, he believes, is to uphold the framework of law and order within which an individual can choose for himself what is in his best interests, without being coerced by others. Attempts by the State to deliver social justice would require a form of bureaucratic planning which would turn citizens into clients of the State, into latter-day serfs.

It is an important and serious argument which strikes a chord with many people who are not Government supporters. It is also of course the philosophy of the Prime Minister herself. Her famous remark that there is no such thing as society, only individuals, is an expression of the Hayekian view in epigrammatic form.

The practical implications of this philosophy were spelled out in the second Manifesto of the Conservative Selsdon Group in 1977: 'What the public wants should be provided by the market and paid for by people as consumers rather than by tax-payers ... the function of Government should not be to provide services but to maintain the framework within which markets operate.'

A parallel strand of thought became linked to this theoretical analysis. Some American economists like Milton Friedman argued that control of inflation should be the principal objective of any Government, and that that could best be achieved by control of the money supply – broadly the notes and coins in general circulation and the amount that banks have lent their customers – and the reduction of spending on public services to that which could be financed by rates and taxes without printing more money.

Friedman's thinking is the converse of Hayek's: it lacks a solid theoretical *a priori* foundation. An extreme empiricist, he is said by his critics to have elevated one simple relationship to the level of a theory. This has not prevented him from winning supporters. President Reagan paid public homage to the need to restore a 'good housekeeping' economic strategy based on balanced budgets and sound money. While in office Reagan did not apply that strategy to the United States economy, but contented himself with advising America's trading rivals, like Great Britain, of its merits. Friedman's analysis was given prominence in this country during the 1970s by the Institute of Economic Affairs, and gained support amongst economists, financial journalists and ultimately leading figures in the Conservative Party, then in opposition. The influence of the two traditions can clearly be seen in 'The Right Approach to the Economy', which declared, in 1977: 'Our intention is to allow state spending and revenue a significantly smaller percentage slice of the nation's annual output and income each year.'[3]

In practice, Professor Hayek's work and that of Milton Friedman did not originally seem relevant to education, but with the freeing of economic life from Government intervention Hayek's ideas were interpreted in a way which foreshadowed the education debate. The Hayekian approach was already well entrenched within Whitehall. When Francis Cripps, the Cambridge economist, and I worked as advisers at the Department of Industry, we noticed with fascination that the day-to-day advice given by civil servants to Ministers (for example in relation to companies in danger of bankruptcy) was quite inconsistent with the guiding principles of Labour's industrial policy, which emphasised the Government's responsibility to intervene in and plan our industrial life. This was the case even when officials were genuinely sympathetic to the Secretary of State's policy. We resolved, therefore, to analyse the separate pieces of written advice, in order to determine the system of thought that underlay them and to discuss it with the civil servants.

A reading of the various documents revealed a controlling philosophy with which Professor Hayek would have been wholly in sympathy. The role of Government was to act as a referee in industrial life, but not to intervene. If a company was facing bankruptcy it should be allowed to collapse, and its assets freed for involvement in another more successful enterprise. The process of industrial life and death was in essence a natural process which Government should not override unless there were powerful reasons of State. If the Department of Industry remained true to this policy of inactivity, our manufacturing industry would grow healthily by its own natural mechanisms.

The senior officials at the Department of Industry readily identified this as, broadly, their own picture. We suggested that we should look out of the window of the Department, so to speak, to see whether the process was working as envisaged. This suggestion was rejected absolutely and with deep emotion. We had identified a philosophical system and, in addition, a faith, which was superior to the evidence.

What made the issue even more complicated to discuss was that, though officials passionately believed in the Hayekian approach in principle, they actually applied a policy of discretionary subsidy: their major objective was to ensure that when public money was invested in a company the Government did not buy shares as a private investor would have done, but offered the money as a loan or a grant. Confusion often resulted: for example, when Eric Varley became Secretary of State for Industry in 1975, he had not had time to decode the complex double-talk that characterises public life. Faced with the likelihood that Chrysler might go bankrupt, and understanding that the Department, and indeed the Government, was publicly opposed to backing lame ducks, he confidently recommended that the company be allowed to collapse. His Cabinet colleagues gazed at him incredulously, and rejected his advice. Another Minister, Harold Lever, was placed in charge of the rescue operation. Varley, mortified, offered his resignation, but it was refused.

This ambivalent relationship between philosophy and practice was to reappear in the education debate.

Hayek and Friedman were really the co-godparents of Kenneth Baker's Education Act. But the theory behind the legislation was developed over a period of years by a small group of British academics, associated with a famous series of polemical publications known as the Black Papers,[4] with the Conservative theoretical journal *The Salisbury Review*, and with individual pamphlets such as the Omega Report.[5]

Among the leading figures was Dr Rhodes Boyson, originally a London head teacher, now a Member of Parliament and Government Minister. Brian Cox, Professor of English at Manchester University edited Black Paper One with his colleague A. E. Dyson. Professor Cox is now Chairman of the Government Working Party on the teaching of English in primary schools. Baroness Caroline Cox, lecturer at North London Polytechnic and later Director of the Centre for Policy Studies, founded by Mrs Thatcher, wrote regularly, as did Roger Scruton, Professor of Aesthetics at Birkbeck College in London.

This group, who were widely ridiculed at the time, wrote, campaigned and argued for their evolving vision of a reformed education service until, in 1988, twenty years after the publication of the first Black Paper, their vision became reality.

From the beginning their project differed from that of Hayek. He was concerned, at least ostensibly, with the economic liberation and dignity of the individual and the avoidance of 'serfdom'. The Black Paper writers were concerned to maintain the traditional social order. This less energetic vision contained within it the acceptance of the existence of a socially deprived class for which, in reality, a separate education was planned. This distinction was clear to at least one of the writers. When I debated, with Paddy Ashdown, against Kenneth Baker and Roger Scruton at the Oxford Union in 1987, Scruton reproved a student who described him as a monetarist. He was, he said, uninterested in the issues of economic liberalism and monetarism: 'I am correctly to be described as a reactionary,' he explained.

Ultimately it was the fusion of Hayek's vision of individual freedom with Friedman's monetarist economic thesis and with the Conservative acceptance of a hierarchically structured society that produced Kenneth Baker's revolutionary plan. The internal tension between the fused elements remains.

The Black Paper writers were stirred into action by disturbances in the universities in the late sixties. Students at the London School of Economics and in art colleges like Hornsey were engaged in a series of disruptive disputes with college authorities over their working conditions, curriculum and the decision-making structures of college life. The disputes spread to other universities. In addition, many students were involved in wider protest movements on such issues as the war in Vietnam and Britain's continued commercial dealings with the South African regime.

The agitation amongst students at that time was so extensive that people of widely disparate views believed that a permanent alteration to the existing political order was taking place. Theorists of the left suggested that the students, sons and daughters of the proletariat, receiving first-generation university education, were a revolutionary class which would precipitate the overthrow of the established order. Supporters of that order feared a similar outcome. After all, in France student protest had nearly brought about the fall of the Government; in the USA the protest movement stopped President Johnson from running for re-election.

I was working at the National Union of Students during this period with the new, radical President, Jack Straw, today a Member of Parliament. From our vantage point the level of concern or optimism appeared exaggerated. But to many the stability of the education service seemed to be undermined, and the consequences of egalitarian principles appeared more threatening to the political order than had ever been imagined. Timothy Raison wrote: 'A common malaise runs right through our present education; the roots of student unrest are to be found as early as the primary school.'[6] Angus Maude's opinion was that the most serious danger facing Britain was 'the threat to the quality of education at all levels. The motive force behind this threat is the ideology of egalitarianism.'[7]

This was the atmosphere in which the collection known as the Black Paper was published in March 1969. It caused a sensation.

The writers first set out to prove that equality was impossible. 'More means worse', was their response to the expansion of university places recommended by the Robbins Report. They argued that society was arranged into social classes with different incomes and resources because children were born with differing levels of intelligence which the educational process could not affect.

'There are two principal reasons why working class children on average do worse than middle class children,' wrote Richard Lynn, one of the authors. 'One is that they are innately less intelligent on average and the other is that their families provide a less suitable milieu for scholastic success. Neither of these will be changed to any appreciable degree by abolishing independent and grammar schools.'[8]

Certainly, they acknowledged, some working-class

children were as innately intelligent as most middle-class children. Geniuses were occasionally born to poor households. 'Gauss, the greatest mathematician of all time, was the son of a German bricklayer, La Place of a French farm labourer; Kepler's father was a drunken innkeeper; Kant's a strapmaker.'[9] In general, however, intelligence was hereditary, and corresponded with social class. The high level of innate ability of parents who have entered the professions 'tends to be transmitted to their children'. Educational efficiency naturally pointed to a school system organised along stratified lines recognising that intelligence was so distributed. Where intelligence at variance with this pattern occurred in individuals, selection tests or other devices should be used to identify and promote the relevant children.

The view that the distribution of intelligence underlay the broad organisation of social classes was later applied by Anthony Flew and others to support the contention that there was no systemic racial discrimination in the United Kingdom, but in all probability a genetic variation between ethnic groups: 'No one is so rash as to dispute the genetic determination of the racial and hence biological defining characteristics, so we can have little reason for confidence that there is no significant difference in the distribution of the other genes.'

Lack of ability was thus the cause of scholastic under-achievement. Efforts to bring more black and ethnic minority people into senior positions in our society by positive discrimination would lead to social injustice 'even if there are even average differences of genetic endowment'. The consequence would be severe over- and under-representations.

The education of girls was not discussed separately in the first Black Paper. However, the basic case for the inherent abilities of girls is stated in the second paper, in 1969, 'The Mental Differences Between Children', which quotes a study of the ablest pupils in a selected group of comprehensive schools. The investigator reports that the schools made no provision for subjects for which pupils had special aptitude and ability, namely higher mathematics, nuclear physics and molecular biology for boys and poetry, painting and ballet dancing for girls.

The truth, for these writers, was that the organisation of social classes arose out of the merits of the individuals concerned. Efforts to ensure greater equality simply led to a diminution of quality: worse, they threatened the social order itself with instability.

The establishment of this 'truth' about the nature of children led to a review of educational needs, and an acceptance of the inevitability of inequality and social class gave rise to fresh objectives. The first was the need to 'civilise and discipline' the new rich: 'The public schools are again socially relevant, they are needed to save us from the aristocracy of tycoons,' wrote Donald McLachlan in 1969. Not only did the public schools need preserving for the children of the 'large new class pushing its way up to wealth and status', but new schools were needed. McLachlan advocated 'a number of specially designed independent day schools, located in the growth points of business and industrial life . . . providing the competition that local authority schools should face'. He continued: 'These public day schools founded by private enterprise, offering education on hire purchase . . . might have boarding wings.'[10] His words outlined the rationale of the institutions that were, twenty years later, to be known as City Technology Colleges (CTCs).

The Black Paper writers also argued that the restoration of traditional teaching styles and traditional standards of achievement should replace the pursuit of equality, because by comparison with the legendary achievements of children of long ago, present-day schools were failing. Standards, Cox and Dyson declared in 1969, were 'lower than they were fifty-five years ago just before the 1914 –1918 war'. In support of this contention they compared the mathematical problems children were tackling by the age of 12 in the 1920s to what was being asked of a similar age group in the present day. The reason for this drop in standards, they suggested, was a widespread abandonment of traditional objectives. In post-war infant schools, they said, 'it has been considered slightly old fashioned to teach reading at all'.[11]

The pursuit of equality, as a philosophy, was to blame, together with a contemporary lack of respect for authority and a refusal to take responsibility: modern education 'disintegrates the standards and structures on which education depends. It is a levelling down process, actively unjust to brighter children and dangerous for the nation as a whole'. Above all, they said, standards were threatened by a modern fear of acknowledging the difference between pupils, by testing or examining. The result was disorder, lax discipline and a failure to achieve, endemic throughout our schools, and in particular in comprehensive schools.

Why was this situation being tolerated by those in charge? They argued that education had suffered from 'producer capture'. It was being run in their own interests by an educational élite of bureaucrats and teachers indifferent to the needs of the consumers – parents and children, despite vast expenditure. Education spending had doubled in real terms between 1944 and 1979/80, at a time when the diminishing birth rate was reducing the number of children. Baroness Cox said the 'pied pipers'[12] of education could give no evidence to substantiate their claim that there had been an improvement in standards, or even that smaller classes made for more effective as opposed to more agreeable teaching. Worst of all, they believed that these educational élites suppressed the evidence of their own failures – examination results, truancy rates. Labour councillors, they said, preoccupied themselves with political interference in the schools while colluding with the professionals in covering up unpalatable truths about performance.

The answer to this bold and iconoclastic vision, true to

Hayek's analysis in *The Road to Serfdom*, was to break up the bureaucracies to free the schools from the clutches of the local authority planners and make them compete by placing them in the market environment of parental choice. Taxpayers' money was being wasted: the answer was to reduce the level of public money going into the schools and to reintroduce parental fees. The teacher-producers could not be trusted. Very well then, parents should run the schools. The Government would decide what was taught in every school and devise tests which all children would take at regular intervals throughout their school life.[13] Ideally, schools should receive no direct public funds at all: parents should be given vouchers to 'spend' at the school of their choice.

This Hayekian vision of empowering the people, as individuals, to choose was embellished by the authors' own commitment to the maintenance of a hierarchical and traditional society. So the foundation of new kinds of schools – City Technology Colleges – was supported; tax-payers' money should be used to help parents who wished to switch from State schools to private schools to do so. All parents who could afford to pay at least a proportion of the cost of their children's education should be financially supported and encouraged to move out of the State sector, which would remain for those who literally could not afford to pay.

This, broadly, was the analysis, critique and solution to the needs of the British education service adopted by Mr Baker in 1988, forty-four years after the 1944 Education Act and the publication of *The Road to Serfdom*, twenty years after the publication of 'A Fight for Education: a Black Paper'.

The plan reflected in the Education Reform Act is based on a philosophy, a faith, and a commitment to a particular kind of society. The system of schooling it is intended to replace was based on a very different philosophy. Had the established system failed?

TWO

The Egalitarian Dream

Most people can vividly remember their first day at secondary school: I know I do. Weeks before, my mother, standing at the step, had opened the official envelope and told me that I had passed 'the scholarship' as the 11+ examination was then known. From that day, life turned into a kind of Cinderella story: letters arrived for my parents telling them to buy me hats and hockey boots, a braid-edged blazer from a very classy store, indoor shoes and outdoor shoes, a gym slip with a pocket, a tennis racquet and a purse to be kept on my person at all times. So awed were my parents by this equipment list that they withdrew their savings and obeyed the instructions to the letter. The whole summer was spent packing and unpacking these purchases until finally, laden with this improbable booty, I staggered into my new school. It seemed, by comparison with where I lived, to be a most beautiful building, with polished parquet floors – remember the indoor shoes – a library, quietly spoken staff, and classrooms with French windows that opened onto balconies looking over gardens, trees and the hockey pitch to the River Ouse.

Since I left my school I have not always conformed to its more sacred tenets. I have eaten fish and chips in the street. My purse has not remained 'on my person at all times' to avoid putting temptation in others' way. I have never once pronounced the word 'off' to rhyme with 'wharf' as we were once memorably instructed to do. But I respect the memory of the school and its staff, and I was happy there.

What is not clear to me now, and was not clear to me then, was why in equity and decency only nine of the hundred or so children in the same year as myself at primary school could be given such an opportunity, and why the parents of all the rest should be told their children had 'failed'. This question of whether children, at the age of 11, should be segregated into groups on the basis of parental income, or test scores, and given different educations, differently financed and on different sites, is a pivotal one for British educationists.

The thinkers upon whose work Kenneth Baker relied in fashioning his reformed school system accepted that such inequality was inevitable. For them the attempt by Governments since 1944, in partnership with local authorities, to plan an education service which genuinely offered equal opportunity to all had been an expensive bureaucratic failure. The decision in 1965 to establish comprehensive secondary schools, each of which would be attended by a cross-section of the child population, was the signal for a counter revolution.

But what was the system's record really like? And were its critics correct in saying that it had failed so drastically that it needed to be completely replaced?

The 1944 Education Act was itself a compromise: it came before the House of Commons when the end of the Second World War was in sight. A programme for building a better Britain was being drawn up. After many months of back-room negotiation the first part of that programme, the plan for the reconstruction of the education service, had been completed by 'Rab' Butler, President of the Board of Education in the wartime coalition Government.

It was obviously a negotiated programme. The churches were being allowed to retain control of the day to day administration of their schools. Daily assembly was required and religious education had to be taught. But, in a historic step, the Government took the power, and accepted the duty 'to promote the education of the people' and to provide 'a varied and comprehensive educational service in every area'.[1]

Another important decision was to provide economic equality of opportunity. Parents were not to be charged fees. Government was to pay half the cost of the school system, and local councils were to pay the balance out of rates. The system was to be free at the point of use. A third key decision was that the system was to be run as a partnership between central Government and local authority – a national service locally administered. Elected local authorities (LEAs) were to be responsible for their own areas.

The Bill envisaged education for the whole child: meals and milk, medical inspections, leisure and sporting facilities. It intended to expand the education service so that every child stayed at school until 16. Beyond that age county colleges were planned to provide further education for all, and nursery schools envisaged.

The spirit of the Bill was egalitarian, requiring that each child be educated according to age, ability, and aptitude and promising free secondary education for all. Butler recognised that 'equality of opportunity would remain something of an empty phrase if children entered the period of compulsory schooling from conditions of family deprivation'.[2]

Enthusiastic speeches greeted Butler's proposals. 'This Bill,' said Sir Roger Shakespeare, Member for Norwich, 'is a comprehensive measure which gathers up the dreams of all educational reformists and the first Bill that deals with the whole of the educable life of the child from the nursing age . . . to university and adult education.'[3]

It was a revolution by consent, uniting powerful forces in society. Government, big business and powerful trade unions had planned the war effort together and expected to plan the peace. All supported the education programme, which seemed to combine equal access to education for

individual children with a plan which met society's antici-
pated needs in a manner consistent with the economic
philosophy of the time.

The planning and thinking did not stop there. The
rollcall of Committees and Enquiries, Reports and Circu-
lars over the years is exhausting even to enumerate. But
several landmarks stand out, especially in the 1960s and
early 1970s. In 1963 a committee chaired by Lord Robbins
looked into higher education[4] and made the then revolutionary recommendation that every qualified student
should have the right to a college or university place. The
Conservative Government accepted this proposal within
twenty-four hours.

John Newsom investigated the education of children of
average ability between the ages of 13 and 16. His 1963
report, 'Half Our Future',[5] showed that these students
were held back by social factors, educated in inferior
buildings and received less than their fair share of resources. He recommended that the school leaving age be
raised to 16. Margaret Thatcher, while Education Minister, did so nine years later.

The Plowden Report on primary education in 1967[6]
recommended that educational priority areas be created so
that schools in regions inhabited by poor families would
receive extra financial help. In 1968 this too was done.

In 1972, Margaret Thatcher asked local authorities to
provide nursery education for half of all 3-year-olds and
90 per cent of 4-year-olds.[7]

The motive power of the vision of equality in education
was thus maintained for many years. Much was achieved,
but, in contemplating the record of four decades of planning, one very obvious point stands out. The 1944 Act was
never fully implemented. It took nearly thirty years to raise
the school leaving age to 16. The system of county colleges
was never realised. The local authorities did not set up a
nursery education sector. There was a sense in which that
first vision, which had so inspired the House of Commons,

was not seriously put to the test. This was partly because of the effort and resources needed for basic provision. It is difficult, looking back, to envisage the scale of the task facing those responsible for implementing the '44 Act in the years after the war. First, the whole infrastructure of planning had to be created. In 1902 there were 315 local education authorities in England and Wales. Some of these were responsible for about twenty elementary schools and perhaps two or three schools catering for secondary-age students. Many would have employed only one professional educational administrator. The 1944 Act reduced the number of authorities to 154. They were allocated geographically sensible areas to plan and given the managerial powers to administer education provision within them. But the recruitment of a network of professional education managers at local level took time. Since it is difficult to plan without planners, progress towards the promised land of equal opportunity for all was slowed down.

Combined with the need to recruit managers was the need for new buildings. During the six years of war, 5,000 schools had been destroyed or damaged and there had been no building during that time. In 1947 the school leaving age was raised to 15 and there was a huge post-war increase in births. There was a desperate need for a building programme of unprecedented proportions. By 1952 the first thousand schools had been built. By 1970 there were approximately 12,000 new schools, 5.6 million new places and a school population of 8 million.

The investment of time, money and optimism that went into the building programme was prodigious. The imagination and energy that fired the programme was born of a partnership between the architects, planners and bureaucrats of the Ministry of Education and those of the local authorities. At the time, the programme appeared to be a triumph of planning, but mistakes were made. The schools were built in accordance with strict Government regulations and cost limitations. Later it was realised that, in the desire to save money, the building methods were in many cases second-rate, so that new schools expected to cater for future generations, constructed on loans repayable by local authorities over sixty years, started to deteriorate, while pre-war buildings needed maintenance.

The worst blunder was the reliance on the pattern of schooling from the past as the basis for the egalitarian programme of the post-war world. In 1944 there were already three types of school. Grammar schools, that had come into existence 'for teaching grammatically the learned languages', had gradually evolved into academic schools that prepared children of the professional classes for university. Technical schools of various kinds had evolved out of the British fear of European industrial competition in the 1870s. Elementary schools had evolved out of charitable and church initiatives to provide an education for the children of the poor.

'There were three strands of secondary education in 1900,' says the Ministry of Education Report for 1950. They were the grammar school, the elementary school and the technical school. These strands were distinguishable in the Schools Inquiry Commission of 1868,[8] and the pattern of their evolution was clearly visible in the hundred years during which responsibility for providing popular education was gradually transferred from voluntary effort to statutory authorities, and from ecclesiastical to secular direction, while the funding of the service shifted from charitable sources to taxation and rates.

How did the pattern of the past become the model for the post-war period? The Act suggested no prototype for the style of school that should be introduced. Naturally, therefore, it could not indicate, even in the broadest terms, what should be taught, or comment on the appropriate teaching method.

The 1945 Labour Government, cautious and conservative despite its enormous majority, simply defined what the Act said about education according to age, ability and aptitude as requiring three different kinds of school for three different kinds of child, each of whom would be identified by an intelligence test at 11 years of age. There was no evidence to support this view of the three kinds of children: it just seemed to be right. The local authorities were instructed accordingly and the school system was built from the ruins of war in accordance with it.

Ellen Wilkinson, Labour Minister of Education made the position clear: 'People have said that by talking in terms of three types of school we are promulgating a wrong social philosophy. I do not agree. By abolishing fees in maintained schools we have ensured that entry to these schools shall be on the basis of merit. I am glad to say we are not all born the same.'

'How ideas persist,' wrote the educational historian H. C. Dent in 1952. 'However much social change may appear to constitute a break with the past it is essentially a product of that past. The revolution that is bringing in the Welfare State will greatly change the English people but they will still be the English people ... the basic pattern remains recognisably the same.'[9]

Ellen Wilkinson's decision was in line with the conventional wisdom of the day, but it was a blunder. No one really knew what was to be taught and by what means in these different types of schools. Pamphlets to reassure puzzled parents were produced by the Ministry of Education: they are written in a tremendously optimistic style, but the confusion of the time is very clear. In one such pamphlet, 'A Picture for Parents', published in 1950, the schoolmaster Mr Green tries to describe the system to Mr Jones the postman: ' "The scholarship holders, they're good at their books. Well they go on studying them at the grammar school and that's fair enough. But these . . ." He looked over at his top class and did not finish the sentence. "But the new Act says that they are all to have their chance

– all of them. They're to have their own kind of secondary education – whichever suits them best." '[10]

The timetable of the grammar school was easy enough to decide upon. In 1904 Sir Robert Morant, a civil servant, had issued regulations on the subject as part of his programme for developing 'expert governors or guides, or leaders'. He envisaged that grammar school children should study English language and literature, history and geography, a foreign language, mathematics, science and drawing. It is a perfectly sensible programme in many ways. My own daughter is following exactly such a curriculum for her GCSE at an inner London comprehensive school today.

The grammar schools naturally enough stuck to that prescription. The technical schools – as I can testify since I taught in one – never had the slightest idea what a technical child was, so they too followed the grammar school plan.

80 per cent of children, however, were in secondary modern schools: they were supposedly quite different from the old elementary schools with their unpopular rote learning. They were also supposedly quite different from the grammar schools and technical schools. What were they actually to be like? No one knew.

What was to be taught in the secondary modern was left to the teachers to devise, on a school by school basis. 'A Picture for Parents' describes a staff meeting at the new kind of secondary modern in the country. Mr Wood, the headmaster, addresses the staff: ' "We've got to provide something as full in its way as grammar school education but different. What's it to be?" ' The staff decide: ' "Where does the grammar school education begin? . . . in the schoolroom. Well, we'll begin outside!" And by this beginning he settled the whole future of the school.'[11]

Here was the central core of the secondary modern curriculum and teaching method. Students should learn from experience, by doing. Picture after picture shows children building sheds, caring for rabbits, taking temperatures, making models, collecting specimens from ponds and describing their findings, dissecting rabbits, building rockeries, feeding chickens, keeping bees, shoeing horses, making dresses, examining a tractor, swimming, country dancing, cooking over a campfire, working on a bus, caring for a baby, hanging out washing, ironing, knitting, acting, making toys . . . anything but opening a book. Many schools managed to devise worthwhile work programmes for the children. Many did not, as I can testify as a former teacher.

As a method of providing for the educational needs of 80 per cent of children over the age of 11, it was, in my opinion, a shabby betrayal of the common people who had just fought a war, so they were told, for democracy and a better future. It indicated the shortcomings of British pragmatism and common sense, and wasted the talents of the nation's children.

From the start parents were unappreciative. ' "What does it all amount to?" they asked. "Aren't you, well just playing at it?" '[12] Neither the secondary modern school nor the technical school ever identified the separate work programme or style of teaching which logically derived from the supposedly separate type of child they were teaching.

Under pressure from parents, technical and modern schools began to enter pupils for the public examination system. As the number of entrants rose, so timetables and teaching methods of technical and modern schools converged with those of the grammar schools, though the secondary modern teacher retained a commitment to officially recommended 'learning by doing', which was later to come under ferocious attack. The grammar schools, however, were better resourced than the others, with more teachers and better-equipped buildings. Their pupils performed more successfully in public examinations, and parents were keen that their children should attend them.

Gradually parents came to realise the unfairness of the selection system. For example, the number of grammar school places available varied enormously according to where you happened to live. There were fewer places in working-class areas so poorer children had to do better than middle-class children to win them. Doubts were cast on the validity of the examination itself. It was rumoured that the pioneer of the test, Cyril Burt, had 'cooked the books' and invented figures to support his contention that intelligence was innate and could be measured.

In the end popular revulsion at the idea – even if it was possible – of classifying children so definitively at the age of 11 was the deciding factor. There was a fundamental sense that children deserved not just economic equality – free schooling – but educational equality too. To some, like Harold Wilson, Leader of the Labour Party, that meant that every child should receive a grammar school education: to others that every child should go to a comprehensive school. And what was a comprehensive school? Once again, no one quite knew.

In 1965 Anthony Crosland, the Minister of Education, issued Circular 10/65, requesting local authorities to draw up plans for the provision of comprehensive schools.

This Circular, a watershed in the history of public education, was simply a letter from the Minister of Education to the local authorities. It was not a legally binding document like the 1944 Act. It requested LEAs to draw up plans for the abolition of the 11+ examination and for the provision of comprehensive schools. It defined comprehensives as 'a school community in which pupils over the whole ability range, and with differing interests and backgrounds, can be encouraged to mix with each other, gaining stimulus from the contacts and learning tolerance and understanding in the process'.[13]

More than twenty years after the 1944 Act had been

passed its egalitarian spirit was at last expressed in support of an egalitarian organisational plan – the comprehensive school. But by that time implementing that comprehensive system involved undoing much of what had been achieved in the post-war years. Moreover, the Government refused to provide extra finance for the change. Of the total secondary school stock in 1964, only 189 were comprehensives. By January 1966 there were 342 comprehensive schools, but only about a quarter of them were custom-built. Even in 1969, three quarters of the comprehensives were adapted from grammar schools, technical schools, or secondary modern schools.[14] Those councils which had been most zealous in building to the specifications of 1945 found themselves faced in 1965 with expensive buildings which they had still not paid for, standing on separate sites and with overlapping or duplicated facilities which now had to be reordered into a new comprehensive secondary system.

Within the schools the majority of teachers had been trained for the old elementary system or for the tripartite system. Some had been among the 350,000 emergency teachers trained after the war. Some had diplomas from teacher training colleges. Some were graduates without teaching qualifications, some with. Most had developed specialisations within the tripartite structure or had been trained by lecturers whose only teaching experience had been in the old élitist organisations. Twenty years of building and teacher training had been devoted to providing for the wrong plan.

Even as the education planners wrestled to repair the strategic blunders of the past, they were confronted with new crises. It was as if the gods had a sense of humour. The annual birth-rate began to decline sharply. At first, in the early seventies, this decrease was dismissed as a demographic hiccup. It took several years for the truth to sink in. The number of pupils in our schools was going to decrease by as much as a third. Suddenly there were too few children to fill the classrooms. Yet facilities were still inadequate and class sizes too large. It was a planner's nightmare. A first response was to suggest that the fall in rolls should simply lead to smaller classes and better facilities. It was not to be. For the annual drop in the birth-rate was not spread evenly across the country. It varied from area to area, from district to district, and over time.

In areas like London, for which I was responsible from 1981 to 1987, the drop in birth-rate had been early and drastic. A ten-year review of secondary schools resulted in 53 being closed – over a quarter of the secondary schools in London. The strain, insecurity and stress involved in this process dominated the service. A typical amalgamated school with 180 first-year students would have been formed from three former schools on separate sites which between them had been planned to take over 400 students in the first year. The merging of these schools was a task of enormous complexity, for which councillors like Margaret Morgan, the professional administrators (like Peter Newsam, the ILEA Chief Education Officer) and London teachers have never been given full credit.

In addition to all this, the children themselves began to change. Beginning in the fifties, Britain was gradually transformed into a multiracial society by the arrival of British passport holders from former colonies. The scale of the change in the population of the inner cities can be judged from the fact that there are now 172 different languages spoken in the homes of London's pupils.

Ethnic minority communities established themselves in the cities and sent their children – British citizens – to the local schools. To Afro-Caribbean and Asian families education was a vital passport to work and to a better life in their new society. They sought an education of quality in the orthodox sense: they also looked for the adaptation of what was being taught, and how it was being taught, to reflect their own cultures.

In the sixties and seventies the role of women in society began to change; more and more women worked, even if they were married and had children. In an analysis similar to that offered by black intellectuals, feminists pointed to the differences in the qualifications achieved by girls and boys, and the 'hidden agenda' in the education girls received.

Equal opportunity, once intended to provide equality irrespective of social class, became associated with the elimination of discrimination against the black and ethnic minority communities and against the female majority. As the social patterns of the population altered, traditional attitudes towards the relations between women and men shifted, bringing sensitive and contentious questions about the role of the teacher to the fore. Educators simultaneously faced a crisis of planning and a new crisis of ideology.

By the early 1970s a fresh question began to pose itself. Unemployment, that dreaded spectre from the thirties had begun to rise, and parents and pupils began again to question the essential purpose of schooling.

Many authorities, even in the 1980s, were still wrestling with these problems, none of them of their own making. The school closure and amalgamation programme was still being carried through to create a network of schools of the right size with appropriate facilities for the pupils in its area. In London, following riots in Brixton, the needs of the black and ethnic communities had become particularly urgent. The need to make a success of the comprehensive system by defining its goals, measuring its achievements and involving all pupils and parents was being researched, and the shadow of youth unemployment was affecting the sense of purpose of the whole system.

So had the whole post-war educational effort been an expensive bureaucratic failure? Should the faults of the system be laid at the door of the producers – the planners and teachers – who consciously or unconsciously worked in their own interests rather than those of the consumer, the parent?

There is a germ of truth in these criticisms, which I shall come to later. But I think a historical account reveals that the educationists who created the post-war system worked within a desperately difficult framework. First, they had to build schools and train teachers on an emergency basis in the aftermath of war. Then they faced demographic changes – the rise then the fall in birth-rate and the altering composition of our society – which no one predicted but to which they in particular had to respond. At the end of the twenty-year period during which the secondary system had been established according to one set of instructions, they were required to transform it into a different system without incurring new expenditure. And they worked without the provision of a coherent intellectual analysis at national level of the education appropriate to the majority of the school population. Viewed against that perspective the achievements of the administrators, planners and teachers command respect.

Did they ever deliver equality of opportunity? Not really, but it was not their fault. Free schooling was provided for by the 1944 Education Act and the fiscal and administrative arrangements that underpinned it. But the secondary system was selective, and what was to be taught was in most cases left to each individual school. In 1965 the Government decided to establish a comprehensive system, but within a few years the economic strategy upon which equality depended began to be abandoned by central Government. From the mid-seventies those trying locally to deliver an egalitarian system of education came more and more to resemble people attempting to run up a down escalator.

THREE

The Party's Over

The withdrawal of British forces from the Suez Canal in 1956 after the threat of financial sanctions by the United States marked the public recognition that Britain had become a second-rank power and could no longer unilaterally make war. Twenty more years elapsed before the further awareness seeped in that Britain, with its economy in relative decline, could no longer unilaterally decide its own economic policy either. The announcement in May 1975 by Tony Crosland, Secretary of State for the Environment, that 'at least for the time being, the party's over' and that public spending was to be constrained was probably the first public warning of the implications.

The visit to London in December 1976 by representatives of the International Monetary Fund to agree the terms under which they would lend money to the British Government to help it avert further sterling crises marked a watershed in, among other things, the history of post-war public education. The crisis caused the break-up of the cross-party alliance that had, since 1945, supported the public funding of services such as education and health.

The national strategy that had been adopted by the post-war Labour Government had been expansionist. It had aimed at rebuilding manufacturing industry, the maintenance of full employment, the provision of social security and the creation of a more equal society. Public spending was the fulcrum of this strategy. It enabled the Government to manage the economy and maintain full employment. Spending on education was part of a plan to achieve greater social equality, and to meet society's need for skilled workers. Because the strategy commanded support across the political spectrum it was broadly maintained during the Conservative Party's periods of office. Sustained reductions in public spending were of course tantamount to the abandonment of the whole strategy. In the event that was what happened.

When the pound began to fall in value in March 1976, several different proposals were put forward. The divisions that opened up that year between the supporters of the various approaches established the political faultlines that endure in the House of Commons today.

On the left, Tony Benn argued for the rejection of the IMF loan and the maintenance of an independent economic policy with existing levels of public spending. His alternative economic strategy based on import controls had been presented to the Cabinet a year previously in a paper written by Francis Cripps and myself in opposition to an earlier round of spending cuts.

Tony Crosland, then Foreign Secretary, advocated the minimum level of spending reductions necessary to satisfy the IMF, currency speculators and the monetarist US Treasury Secretary William Simon, and the maintenance of the post-war strategy at a more constrained level. The majority of Cabinet members agreed with him, but he failed to convince the Prime Minister and was unwilling to vote against him in Cabinet. For Crosland, a former Secretary of State for Education, and one of the intellectual architects of the post-war strategy, it was a personal tragedy. One of his supporters, Shirley Williams, then herself Secretary of State for Education later adopted his approach as part of the policy of the newly-formed Social Democratic Party. Like Ted Heath in the Conservative Party and Macmillan before him, she looked to increasing British involvement in the European Economic Community as the major strategic solution.

Prime Minister James Callaghan, supported by his Chancellor Denis Healey, demanded and got Cabinet support for a substantial programme of public spending cuts. These cuts appeared to signal a conversion to a monetarist analysis. 'You cannot spend your way out of a recession,' Callaghan told the Labour Party Conference of September 1976. He was defeated in the General Election of 1979, and with that defeat the last of the egalitarian generation of post-war political leaders passed from office.

The flirtation with monetarism by Callaghan and Healey had strengthened the conviction of another former Education Minister, Margaret Thatcher, then in opposition. When she succeeded them in office she was determined to maintain an independent economic policy and to conquer inflation by controlling the money supply and drastically reducing public spending. In the event, North Sea Oil revenues strengthened the external financial position. After inflicting a severe deflation during her first term of office, Mrs Thatcher turned away from monetarism. By this time a Government disinvestment programme in education was under way. It was to continue after the rationale for starting it had been abandoned. Indeed disinvestment and privatisation replaced monetarism as the principal objectives of Mrs Thatcher's administration. This whole process is lucidly analysed by William Keegan, Economics Editor of the *Observer*, in his book *Mrs Thatcher's Economic Experiment*, which describes how the monetarists 'failed in their monetarism: they could not control the money supply . . . and the causal connection between the money supply and inflation they believed in did not exist'. Paradoxically, this discovery created an obsession with the one area of the economy where spending could be controlled, the public sector. 'The obsession with the PSBR (Public Sector Borrowing Requirement) was fomented not only by monetarism but also by its failure: the PSBR became the one thing the Government found it could keep down. The commonplace that some public spending was wrong and wasteful . . . became transposed into the conclusion that all public spending (except on defence, law and order etc.) were *a priori* suspect.'[1]

Looking back to 1976 it is possible to trace clearly the disinvestment programme that flowed from the monetarist policies first of Callaghan and Healey, and subsequently of Margaret Thatcher. The fabric of our school buildings deteriorated as a result of the slump in capital spending – that is, spending on new buildings or on major improvements to old ones. The total capital spending of local authorities on housing, roads, parks and schools has been halved in real terms since the mid-seventies. Within that, capital spending on all education projects has come down by two thirds, from £2,022.22 million in 1975/76 to £692.07 million in 1985/86. (The figures are at 1986/87 prices.)

Table 1: Local Authorities' Capital Expenditure, United Kingdom (as percentage of GDP)

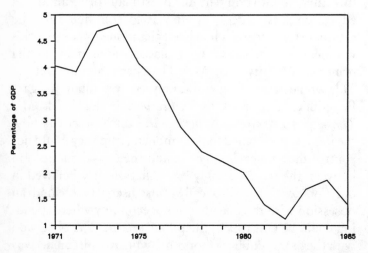

Source: S. Smith and D. Squire, *Local Taxes and Local Government* (The Institute for Fiscal Studies, 1987)

There are 27,513 schools in England and Wales, providing education for approximately 8 million children. The fixed assets – schools, buildings, land, equipment and furniture, probably have a replacement value of about £50 billion. A business would probably think it normal to allocate 2 or 3 per cent of the value of its capital stock each year for renewal of those assets. For schools that would represent a figure of £1,000 million to £1,500 million a year. In England and Wales we have been allocating only £300 million for all capital spent on schools – just 0.5 per cent of its capital value.

Innumerable reports have indicated that the years of capital control have produced drastic deterioration, which would require hundreds of millions of pounds to put right. In 1987 Her Majesty's Inspectorate said: 'The unsatisfactory state of many buildings which has been reported for a number of years persists and in some cases continues to deteriorate. In a fifth of all classes seen in schools, a similar proportion to that recorded last year, accommodation is judged to be having adverse effects on the quality of work, usually because of its unsuitability for specialist use or its poor condition . . . increases in the intervals in the redecoration programme . . . widespread concern about the state of the furniture (which has) reached the end of its useful life with no prospect of replacement.'[2]

For years now local councillors have had the unenviable task of trying to choose between the needs of, say, a primary school with outdoor lavatories that freeze every winter against those of a girls' school in need of laboratory facilities, or with a leaking roof, or both. Or funds for a nursery school have had to be argued for in competition with bids for the cost of rehabilitating severely dilapidated council flats.

This slump in spending has coincided with the fall in the numbers of the child population, which has meant that all over the country, schools have been closed and sold by local councils. Surely those sales could have provided a sensible source of income for the renovation and replacement of existing buildings.

The Audit Commission has publicly said that part of the problem is that not enough schools have been closed and sold.[3] They may be right. But they do not draw public attention to the fact that, despite a critical deterioration in the school building stock, the Government has placed restrictions on the spending of the proceeds from the sale of surplus schools on improving run-down stock still in use. At the same time, the Government has tightly controlled the borrowing capacity of local authorities.

When major public building works are undertaken, the money may be borrowed by local authorities in much the same way as a householder taking out a mortgage to finance an extension to his house, or a private company borrowing to finance an expansion of its premises or the opening of new ones. The reason for borrowing is similar in each case. The sum of money involved is too large to be found from the revenue, or income or profits from a single year, but can comfortably be paid off over several years.

This is what monetarism has meant for education in practice. While householders and private companies have been free to borrow as much as they can persuade a bank or a building society to lend them, and during a period when financial institutions have been engaged in a cut-throat competition to lend, local authorities have been forbidden to borrow and have thus been prevented from spending the necessary amount on State school building, on the grounds that by *not* doing so they were promoting the economic prosperity of the country. The reductions in capital spending, combined with alterations to the arrangements for day-to-day revenue funding, amounted to an undeclared policy of repealing the 1944 Education Act by stealth.

When 'Rab' Butler introduced his Education Bill for its final reading in the House of Commons in the year preceding the end of the war, he promised Members that the

Government would pay over half the day-to-day or revenue cost of the school service out of national taxation, increasing the proportion in areas with greater need. Over the years, the percentage share of the cost of local spending including statutory schooling met by Government rose to 66.5 per cent. Since 1979, however, Government has steadily reduced the proportion of its contribution to approximately 45 per cent.

A graph prepared for Jack Straw by the House of Commons statistical section shows the gradual alteration in the share of costs between the two partners.

Table 2: Education Expenditure – Schools England
(79/80 PRICES INDEX 79/80 = 100)

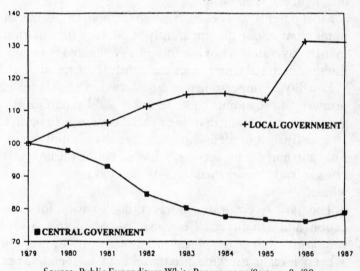

Source: Public Expenditure White Papers, 1979/80 to 1987/88

As Government spending has fallen, that of local authorities has risen to fill the gap. The shift in cash terms has been considerable. In 1979 central Government spent £297 per pupil against the £378 that came out of the purses of the local ratepayers. By the end of 1987, the central Government figure was £487 per head, while the local ratepayers' share had risen to £1,024.

Government Ministers and their supporters have had a splendid time presenting this information. On the one hand, they have publicly congratulated themselves on their careful, indeed parsimonious use of resources and their matching of tax cuts with reductions in public spending. They have attacked local authorities for 'overspending', that is increasing local spending to compensate for the Ministers' cuts. At the same time, they have taken credit for the fact that revenue spending has not fallen – 'The public education service is safe in our hands' – while not revealing that the only reason for the overall maintenance of spending has been the local 'overspending' undertaken in defiance of their wishes.

Most parents will be less concerned about the source of funds than about the apparently reassuring information that the overall level of spending has remained constant. But that national figure hides some disturbing trends.

Equality of opportunity as established in 1944/45 was primarily an economic concept. Every child, whatever the geography of their birth or their social class, was to receive an equally well funded education, free at the point of use. That aim had not in fact been achieved before the financial crisis in 1976. Since then the situation has grown steadily worse.

The most recent HMI report on the Provision for Education and Quality of Response, issued in July 1987, emphasises that geographical variations in provision apply at every level 'in the wide differences in LEAs' spending per pupil as per student; in the suitability and state of accommodation; in the quality and quantity of books, equipment and materials available to schools, colleges, subject departments and classes'.

The quality of education provision that a child receives is today, quite literally, an accident of birth. The most fundamentally egalitarian feature of the arrangements made under the Butler Act was the abolition of fees. The deterioration in school buildings as well as (in many areas) seriously inadequate provision of books and equipment has resulted in pressure on parents to make direct contributions to help equip their local school. HMI report, for example, that in 38 per cent of the primary schools they visited in the course of preparing their 1987 report, parental contributions increased the capitation (books and equipment) allowance by 30 per cent.

They gave examples of a combined first and middle school with 528 pupils whose capitation allowance was £9,630, augmented by parental contributions of £10,000, and another 11–16 comprehensive school of 330 pupils where parents contributed £20,000 compared with a capitation allowance of £19,000.

Table 3: Parental Funds as % of Capitation Received by Schools in 1986 (for primary and secondary schools, 1985 percentage in brackets)

Type of school	less than 10%	11–20%	21–30%	more than 30%
Primary %	28 (15)	19 (22)	15 (20)	38 (44)
Secondary %	77 (66)	15 (25)	4 (5)	4 (5)
Special %	47	—	5	48
Total number of schools (1986)	764	234	138	308

Source: Her Majesty's Inspectorate

In 1988, after a successful court case challenging the right of a school to charge for 'extras', Kenneth Baker provided in his Reform Act for such charges to be made. The inadequacy of funding arrangements has meant the development of fee paying and fund raising. The level of income of the parents at a given school determines how far this is possible, and the shortfall in capital spending is far beyond what has been called the 'jumble sale' economy.

A further cost-cutting exercise has been the attempt to keep teachers' pay rises below the rate of inflation. Whether they have succeeded or not is a matter of dispute. One set of figures for the average annual salaries, adjusted to allow for inflation, of full-time teachers in maintained secondary schools since 1975 is given below:

Table 4: Average Annual Salaries of Teachers in State Secondary Schools 1975–85 (adjusted for inflation)

1975	£10,456
1976	£9,989
1977	£9,290
1978	£8,927
1979	£9,012
1980	£9,045
1981	£10,047
1982	£9,884
1983	£10,102
1984	£10,158
1985	£10,157

Sources: DES Statistics of Education 'Teachers' 1975 to 1985, and Index of Retail Prices.

There are other Government computations starting from different years and using different calculating methods, but whatever figures are used, the consequence of this policy was an extended industrial dispute ending with a pay settlement which is a major reason for the apparent maintenance of spending. Most teachers today remain, at best, on a salary which equates in real terms with what their counterparts were earning a decade ago – but most other salaries have risen in real terms over that period. The teaching profession has not shared in the increase in the nation's wealth. The increasing shortage of teachers in secondary schools, particularly in science, maths, craft design and technology, is perhaps one reflection of the Government's financial policy.

What was the purpose of this disinvestment programme? In 'The Right Approach to the Economy' a pledge was given to 'allow State spending and revenue a significantly smaller percentage slice of the nation's annual output and income each year'. This was part of the plan to reduce 'the rate of growth of the money supply in line with firm monetary targets'.[4]

That pledge is being redeemed. Total public spending on education in 1975/76 was 6.4 per cent of Gross Domestic Product. It has fallen markedly since then. In 1981 it stood at 5.5 per cent of GDP, and in 1985–86 at 4.9 per cent. The theory that control of the money supply was the key to successful management of the economy is no longer seriously argued by most of those who supported it ten years ago. We have been left with a fixed policy of steadily reducing education spending, both in real terms and as a percentage of rising national income.

Government has a duty to be concerned, strategically, with the pattern of local government spending (of which education forms 43 per cent) and with the Government contribution to it. By 1975, 66.5 per cent of all local authority revenue was paid for out of central taxation, an unfortunate balance both for democratic reasons and for reasons of local accountability. At the same time, spending was increasing at a faster rate than the nation's wealth.

The Government's response has been to increase the

cost of local spending to ratepayers. Once every pound of spending on local services attracted, on average, 66.5 pence of Government grant. In 1980 Ministers introduced a block grant system which ensured that the proportion of an authority's spending met by grant was reduced if the authority spent more than the Government considered necessary to provide 'a standard level of service'. Every pound spent up to the 'standard level' attracted a grant of 45p on average. Every *extra* pound spent produced a 'fine' of £2 grant loss. At the same time, the block grant itself was annually reduced.

The Government's penalties had the extraordinary effect of costing ratepayers three times as much as the cost of the provision being made. Finally, in 1984, Parliament passed the Rates Act, which gave Government the power to set limits on the rates which councils in England and Wales could levy. It has had similar powers in Scotland since 1983/84. Most recently, as I shall show, the whole system of local government finance is being changed. One of the objects is to create pressure to keep local spending down.

Ministers have justified their capital disinvestment pro-gramme and the requirements for reduced spending by reference to a search for economic efficiency. Black Paper writers have repeatedly suggested that it is impossible to prove that a given level of expenditure relates to improved performance by pupils in schools.

For years the air has been thick with claims of local authority extravagance. It is right and proper that Govern-ment institutions like the Audit Commission should ensure that public money is spent wisely: moreover, local govern-ment, with nearly 2 million full-time and 1 million part-time employees, accounting for over a quarter of all public expenditure and providing services which cost £45 billion annually, is a huge area to survey.

However, in the words of Noel Hepworth, Director of the CIPFA (Chartered Institute of Public Finance and

Accountancy) in a lecture to the Institute of Economic Affairs in 1988: 'a great disservice is done by confusing lower spending levels with greater efficiency. The simplistic political argument is that high spending equals inefficiency. Expenditure is an input and to make judgements about outputs is the critical factor. For the vast majority of local authority services outputs are extremely difficult to determine.'

I will come to the issue of measuring quality later in the book. So far as the general level of education spending is concerned, it is sufficient to say that the requirement that resources be used efficiently is fair and valid.

But it is also true that expenditure relates to policy choices which reflect ideas of what education should be, and which cannot be translated into performance indicators. For example, every ILEA school had a well-stocked library and every secondary school library had a librarian. That is not the case in most parts of the country. There is no way of measuring the impact of a library.

Again, ILEA had a resource allocation system based on the Education Priority Area Index which measured the level of deprivation of pupils within a school and made specific extra provision to meet these needs, such as providing language teachers for children speaking English as a second language. The poorer an area is, or the more complex the needs of a child, the more costly it will be to provide the resources required. Neither target reductions, nor target expansion provide a philosophy for efficient management resources. What was actually needed was an agreed system of assessing educational performance – and that had not been devised. In those circumstances the expansion programmes of many local education authorities were not efficient. They did not stem from clearly-defined goals and were not subject to monitoring and review.

The Government's contraction programme has not been efficient either. Nothing could be more inefficient than the running down of the infrastructure, the mismanagement of pay negotiations leading to a two-year industrial dispute, and the huge unplanned variation in educational provision now prevalent throughout the country. A private sector management could not survive such a record.

As the Government's demand for annual reductions in spending worked through the system, the fracturing of the egalitarian consensus amongst national political leaders was repeated at local level. Some councils accepted the need to contract. Others raised the rates. Others, by techniques of creative accounting, cooked the books in hope of better times. Some advocated resistance to the point of illegality. The budget became the most important policy event of the year, and in the bitter disputes over council spending many excellent councillors, disillusioned, left office altogether.

By 1987, eleven years after the visit of the IMF to London and the adoption of policies of financial contraction, the statutory system of State schooling, although damaged, was still recognisably the system that had been developed in response to the 1944 Education Act. It was still, in principle, free, even if parents were having to fund-raise. It was still dedicated to economic equality even if, in practice, spending varied geographically, and it was still a broadly equal partnership based on shared responsibility for funding, even though the Government share was falling. Most of the secondary provision was comprehensive.

In 1987, after Margaret Thatcher was re-elected for a third term, changes were made to the funding and management of the service which altered it from a system designed to provide planned economic equality of opportunity to a 'market' system, which in reality was designed to create planned inequality.

FOUR

Money Plans

'Money talks', say the Americans. 'Money whispers', says Marx in *Das Kapital*. I suggest that money plans.

The visual evidence for this simple truth is obvious in any town. A walk through Knightsbridge, for example, will reveal the shops, houses and restaurants that serve the wealthy people who live, work and stay in that area. A Hackney housing estate, by contrast, will probably have immediate access to an off-licence, a pub and a takeaway. The income of those who live and work in an area shapes the commercial facilities available within it.

The 1944 Education Act and the financing arrangements that accompanied it were an attempt to remove schools from the shaping flow of the market. Funded in broadly equal proportions from national taxation and local rates, planned and built by local education authorities in partnership with Government, schools were free to the families that used them and (in theory) equally well built wherever they stood. The 1988 Education Act is intended to reintroduce market principles into the provision of State schools. The Local Government Finance Act of 1988 changes the whole basis of local authority finance.

What will be the implications for economic equality of opportunity? From 1 April 1990 central Government will decide on the level of local spending necessary to meet the community's needs in each area. It will then provide on average 75 per cent of this sum in the form of a grant which comes partly out of national taxation and partly

from a national tax on business (Unified Business Rate –
UBR) – the rate that used to be locally levied and collected.
The balance of the local budget is to come from a flat-rate
charge on each adult in the area, the community charge, or
poll tax.

Each school above a certain size, under the guidance of
its governing body, will be responsible for the management of its budget. This is to be allocated on a formula
basis by the local authority, which will retain responsibility for the local capital budget, that sum of money which
it is allowed by Government to spend annually on major
building works. Schools themselves will be much freer to
decide on the appropriate number of pupils. They may opt
out of the local authority system altogether – subject to
parental consent – and become directly financed by Government. Schools will be expected to compete for parental
custom in the traditional commercial manner.

According to *Campaign*, the magazine of the advertising
industry, Saatchi and Saatchi have been given the responsibility of promoting the Grant Maintained Schools Foundation, the institution described by the magazine as a
'guerrilla band' responsible for persuading parents to opt
out of their local education authority.

The grant maintained sector will not be alone in selling
its wares: it is Government policy to encourage private
schools. They too will wish to advertise their superiority,
and the schemes by which parents can spend a lifetime
saving up for their fees.

The Centre for the Study of Comprehensive Schools, not
to be outdone, has issued a leaflet sponsored by British
Petroleum called 'Schools in the Market Place' advising
each State school how to plan its publicity. Presumably
parents can expect to be sent beautiful prospectuses with
soft-focus pictures of children quietly bowed over their
books or returning tousled and laughing from the playing
fields.

Central Government has decided the standard curriculum that is to be taught in each school, and is responsible for the national testing system that accompanies it. Other detailed regulations have been issued governing such things as provision of information to parents considering placing a child at a school.

The directives standardising the education to be found in each school operate on the same principle as the requirement that all weights and measures must be accurate, or that gold and silver must be hallmarked, or that packaged foodstuffs should display their weight and contents and that a minimum level of hygiene must be observed in shops and restaurants. They offer a minimum protection to the customer within the marketplace, and beyond that the customer must choose, pay, and be responsible for the choice they make. By inference the regulations for publication of information and examination results, for testing, and for ensuring conformity of syllabus provide a minimum protection, but of course beyond that the Government takes no responsibility. Let the buyer beware.

The educational implications of what in management terms can best be described as a franchise system I will come to later in the book. It is the financial arrangements which will shape the pattern of schooling. The overall financial plan would lead in a few years to a three-tier system of private schools, independent partially fee-paying schools, and a State school system providing a minimal service of last resort for parents unable to pay. This is broadly the system the 1944 Act replaced.

The financial arrangements are seriously unstable and will lead to a crisis within a few years. This arises from the likelihood that the Government will continue its policy of allocating an annual grant which is less than the true annual increase in the costs of local services, such as schools. The Chartered Institute of Public Finance and Accountancy has recently examined the implications of this for future levels of community charge. It assumed:

- average annual inflation of 5 per cent
- uniform business rate increases of 5 per cent a year, in line with inflation
- local authority cost increases of 6 per cent a year (wage bills tend to run ahead of the Retail Price Index, and this affects all large employers such as local authorities)
- grant aid increases of 4 per cent a year

If these forecasts prove accurate, and each local authority increases its poll tax to match the shortfall in grant, the present average poll tax of £225 would rise by 1994 −95 to about £410 at today's prices – a compound growth of 9 per cent, almost twice the rate of inflation.

Such an increase would be politically impossible to levy, particularly in those areas inhabited by poorer families. A local authority that could not increase its local income would have no alternative but to reduce its spending and therefore its level of service. The local authority is also responsible for the capital budget, which has been severely restricted by Government for many years. Schools in each area will have to wait a long time before a local authority will be able to pay for major renovations to their buildings.

In these circumstances pressure will be generated within schools to opt out of the local authority system and to negotiate direct with Government in the hope of a better deal. Whatever the level of Government grant, however, the cost will be 'top-sliced' from the local authority's total grant.

If different financial arrangements are to be made for grant maintained schools, they must be decided upon and explained. If the funding system is to be exactly the same for schools that have opted out as for local authority schools, and both sectors are to be continuously starved of funds, it is hard to see the point of providing for schools to opt out unless the purpose is to encourage a higher level of parental contributions to those schools.

The issue that has been fudged by statements about

economic efficiency and the virtues of the market needs to be faced. How should education be paid for, and what are the effects on our children of the alternative systems?

If we lived in a society in which every adult enjoyed a similar income, or even a relatively similar income, and parents received allowances equal to the cost of rearing each child, then on the face of it a simple method of paying for the public education service might be to charge parents direct. This is the method adopted by those who send their children to private sector schools, and it seems, superficially, to combine administrative simplicity with parental choice.

In fact we live in a society in which disparity of income is wide. Since 1945 the gap between incomes has narrowed in the whole of the developed world, but in Britain, during the early years of Mrs Thatcher's administration, this process has been reversed. The fall in unemployment since 1987 has restored the gradual process of equalisation, but the gap remains enormous. In addition, a school system which caters for 8 million children needs planning in a way which a small number of public schools does not – and the State has an interest in what goes on and needs the power of the purse strings to affect that.

There are two philosophical responses to those propositions – one which envisages the State providing a minimum 'safety net' system, another which sees the State as providing the whole service. The first view is held by those, like the radical right, who believe that a socially stratified society is both inevitable and desirable, and who support an élitist system of education, and by supporters of *laissez faire* economics. These two groups advocate partial State funding of a school system run at an economic cost and supplemented by fees.

In part their case rests on principle. Cox and others in the Omega Report argue that payment for a child's education should primarily be related to *use* of the service; stating that: 'It is remarkable that a single person or a

childless couple should pay higher taxes in order to educate other people's children.'[1] Furthermore, they suggest
that as it is the parents and the child who gain from the
schooling in later years, they are the ones who should pay
the initial investment.

The Omega Report favours 'attempting to move those
who can afford to pay for themselves out of the State
system . . . leaving the hard stretched resources of the State
system to be used by those who really need it'.

As a result, State education (which would be confined to
those who could not afford to pay) would only provide
education 'to a minimum standard'. A variety of schemes
such as vouchers or income tax rebates would make it
possible for 'a parent seeking a more specialist education,
an emphasis on different subjects or attitudes or even a
little more status and luxury' to combine the cost of State
education with additional fees from their own income to
purchase education at an independent school.

The system advocated by the architects of the present
changes envisages independent schools for children of the
wealthy, who can afford the fees, with an additional
number of children from the ranks of those who can afford
to top up a state subsidy with private funds. State schools
would provide a minimum education for the rest. This they
argue constitutes a choice 'not just for the rich but to all
sectors of the population'.

If parents were to choose freely in this way, one would
expect new independent schools to be established. This
would raise a major planning problem. These writers do
not accept the need for school buildings to be purpose-
built with appropriate facilities and equipment: 'People
commonly make the mistake of supposing that schools to
be viable must be large, purpose built modern installations
. . . the new independent schools of the future . . . are likely
to be small, perhaps occupying a large country house or a
group of town properties on an ad hoc basis.'

So the eventual effect of the Government measures

could be very similar to the programme advocated in the
Omega Report – and, indeed, very similar to the 1870
system of education in this country. The 1870 Education
Act saw the responsibility of the State as being to 'fill the
gaps' left by private provision. Most schools were still to
be private (voluntary) and to continue to enjoy subsidies
(direct grants) from central Government. 'We do not give
up school fees', Forster, the Education Minister, told
Parliament, '. . . and indeed we keep to the present proportions namely of about one third raised from parents,
one third out of public taxes and one third out of local
funds'. Interestingly, Section 25 of the 1870 Act provided
for free tickets (like vouchers) to help poor parents pay
the fees.

From the 1940s onward those who support the need
to ensure economic equality of opportunity for children
despite disparity of family income have supported the
total funding of the education service out of taxation and
rates, free at the point of use, and have expected the State
to bear the high cost of the building programme and to
plan it.

The belief, by no means confined to socialists but shared
by people of most political persuasions, including Con-
servatives, was that everyone should be able to enjoy a
common standard of service irrespective of their ability to
pay as a necessary part of ensuring equality of opportunity
within society. At the same time, it was accepted that the
money to finance these services should come predominantly from general taxation, levied not according to a
person's use of such services but according to ability to
pay. That those with the highest incomes should bear a
disproportionate share of the costs of providing public
services was an integral part of the design of the system.

Some say that, as a society, we cannot afford the kind of
school system envisaged in 1944: that the cost of the
service is outstripping our ability to pay. They allege that
levels of spending on education and on services like school

meals reflect inefficiency and waste, and that parents, by choosing, contributing and paying fees, will gain both choice and control. But is this true?

In fact as a nation we should have more to spend on schooling than we did in 1944. Average earnings rose by 51 per cent between 1948 and 1984, and have continued to rise. The proportion of our income that we spend on food, drink, fuel and clothing has remained fairly constant. The proportion spent on housing has increased with the rise in owner occupation. The effect, on average, is that there has been a real increase in incomes after tax and after expenditure on basic essentials. Quite simply, people have more to spend.

But there are other factors to take into account. From the 1940s to the 1970s there was a trend towards greater equality of income. This trend has now been reversed to such an extent that the richest 10 per cent of the population now keep more income after tax than the entire bottom 50 per cent of the population. According to the most recent figures, the top 10 per cent of income earners have raised their *share* of total pre-tax income from 26.1 per cent in 1978–79 to 29.5 per cent in 1984–85, and their share of post-tax income from 23.4 per cent to 26.5 per cent. The fall in the share of the bottom half is partly due to low pay rises, but tax changes and the rise in National Insurance contributions have also played a part.

The burden of taxation remains broadly constant: it is the distribution which has changed. Only the top 20 per cent and the second to bottom 10 per cent of the population have increased their share of total post-tax income since 1979. Tax concessions have been concentrated on the top 10 per cent.

Sir Keith Joseph, then Education Minister, was asked in May 1984 why spending on children in the best private schools was higher per head than in State schools. He replied: 'If people choose to give up smoking and send their children to private school they should be free to do so.' The howl of outrage from normally calm parents visibly took him aback.

It has become increasingly clear that couples hoping to provide an independent school education for their children will have to make substantial sacrifices. Invest for School Fees, one of a growing number of companies offering advice in this field, suggest that parents of babies born in 1988 will have to save £70,000 in order to send a child to an independent school from the age of 11. Recent figures on household income in Britain indicate that only the top 20 per cent could possibly afford this.

Many households have enjoyed a genuine increase in disposable income since the war precisely because services like education have been paid for out of taxation. A shift towards private education could not possibly be compensated for by tax reductions (see Table 7, p. 155).

The education service has traditionally been funded from Government grant and rates levied on domestic and commercial properties. Some areas, like London, have had a high commercial rate: others have had a much lower commercial rate, and have therefore qualified for increased government grant.

The uniform business rate will redistribute the high commercial rates collected in areas like London – which also contains many very poor areas – uniformly over the whole country. The poll tax, which will operate as a levy on each adult irrespective of income, will be the principal means of *varying* the local income available to a council to spend on schools.

In poor areas political pressure to keep the poll tax low is bound to be put on local councils because households will not be able to afford to pay. Clearly these households will also be unable to afford fees or fund raising, or to top up tax subsidies which offer special terms to parents to send their children into the private sector. It follows that there will be an intensification of the already large variations in the spending per pupil per head in different regions. The resources available to the children of poor parents will be greatly diminished under this system. School buildings, the books and equipment within them, the number of teachers available and hence the size of classes will gradually and visibly correspond to the income of the community, just as do shops, restaurants and other commercial facilities.

To sum up: as a society, we are half as rich again as we were when the 1944 Act was passed, but in terms of income distribution we are just as unequal. Regionally, and so far as particular communities are concerned, the disparity is even worse. While the Government's income from taxation now comes from different sources, it is just as great in real terms. There seems, therefore, to be no reason for altering the pattern of funding of the education service, and every reason for maintaining it.

Although there are new burdens on the Exchequer, caused for example by the rise in unemployment, the increase in the number of pensioners and single-parent families, in 1989 the Government will still have a projected budget surplus of £10 billion. It could afford to increase education spending.

So what will be the effect of the new financial arrangements?

The private school sector itself will presumably continue to cater for a minority of the population, though that minority may expand if the quality of State education falls and if the Assisted Places Scheme is enlarged. Naturally the wealthiest will buy the best education for their children. Competition for places in the City Technology Colleges will probably be intense and, given the specialised nature of the schools, selective: the schools themselves will choose the entrants. It is likely that the children of the highly motivated, best-informed middle-class parents will be selected to enter the schools, and those parents will dedicate their efforts to fund raising and working to improve the schools.

Within the areas where City Technology Colleges exist, therefore, a second tier of education between public and State schools will be set up. This second tier will include the direct grant schools and grammar schools which already exist. Selectivity and a consequent level of fund raising and fee paying by parents are already common to those schools.

Within the State sector, the variation in poll tax income by area will be a primary determinant of level of provision: that will depend both on the ability of householders to pay and the political willingness of each community to fund education.

The most popular schools will inevitably be those which draw the majority of their pupils from middle-class homes: schools situated in working-class neighbourhoods will not find it easy to compete. Gradually a pattern or ladder of status will develop in the towns and cities, defined not only by the social class of the children in the school but also by the variation in income provided by their parents. Without total State funding and the Butler system of varying the level of Government grant to compensate for variations in local income, what must emerge is a three or four tier education system corresponding in *resource* terms to the income grouping and status of the parents.

In practice, given the proposals to allow schools to administer their own (inadequate) budgets and to choose to spend them on teachers, books or equipment, it is likely that average class numbers will rise, and the provision of books will remain insufficient. In these circumstances such 'luxuries' as full-time librarians, music teachers and English or second language teachers are unlikely to be found in many schools.

The legislation which requires schools to charge for extras will mean that unless parents pay the full cost of, for example, school journeys or individual music tuition, their child will not be able to participate. The implications are obvious. Those children who come from homes where private music lessons, sports training, trips to museums and theatres and holidays abroad are available will suffer less than those children for whom the home cannot make such provision. The differential funding of schools will of itself produce a different curriculum: some children will receive a very basic education while others will be culturally enriched, according to parental income.

Children with disabilities will suffer. The Warnock Report[2] recommended the integration of many categories of children with disabilities into the mainstream school population. This is indeed part of the comprehensive ideal, but it is costly, requiring the physical adaptation of schools and the employment of specialist staff. Within the market framework, such a change would not be cost-effective. It must be imposed as part of a planned system.

Economic equality lay at the heart of the mid-twentieth century consensus on education: Tories like Butler who did not necessarily accept educational equality as found in comprehensive schools nevertheless believed that every child should have an equal economic chance. The new arrangements make no such provision. Inequitable financial arrangements combine individual injustice with, from society's point of view, the waste of talent and intelligence. Children from poor families will suffer, and standards will not be improved. As the next chapter shows, the Black Paper writers justified such inequitable arrangements by arguing that intelligence itself was already inequitably distributed. Is there any truth in that idea?

FIVE

What are Children Capable of?

ILEA used to test all its pupils during their final year at primary school and classify them into broad ability bands. The results were not made public, although parents were usually told. The purpose of the exercise was to help the Authority ensure that each comprehensive school contained pupils of all abilities and social classes.

Every year, more girls than boys achieved the top grade – band one, as it was known. Every year, without telling anyone, those responsible for administering the test would reclassify a proportion of boys from the second band as band one, and move the same number of girls down to band two. The examiners believed that an equal number of boys and girls should achieve the top grade, and that this was so important that the figures had to be changed to fit the idea.

As Chair of the Schools Subcommittee, I recommended in September 1982 that we should tell pupils their correct scores, even if it meant admitting that girls, as a group, performed slightly better in the tests than boys. Some members of the committee were extremely unhappy about the change, but in the end it was agreed.

Fortunately, in London, the incorrect banding did not seem to have had any significant effect on the boys and girls concerned, though simply telling girls that they had performed less well in a test than they actually had was malpractice.

But in some local authorities there was still an examination at 11 which determined whether pupils went to grammar or secondary modern school. These test figures too were adjusted so that an equal number of boys and girls were represented in the top ability range. As a result some girls were refused admission to grammar schools despite having test scores higher than some of the boys who were admitted. In 1988 the Northern Ireland Equal Opportunities Commission took the Department of Education and the Western and Belfast Education and Library Boards to court, accusing them of direct discrimination under the Sex Discrimination Act. They won – and 860 girls were given grammar school places as a result.[1]

This kind of thinking is not confined to education. A recent article about pony clubs in the *Daily Telegraph* reveals that although girls 'have an instinctive sympathy with ponies, are less easily scared' and bounce back into the saddle after a tumble, they may be 'barred from the polo teams to give the boys a chance to shine'.[2]

I mention these examples of thinking about girls and boys to show how hard it is for any of us to decide rationally what children are really like, what they are capable of achieving and what they should be given a chance to do. The picture we have in our heads is so powerful that often we would rather blank out information that contradicts it than change the picture itself.

The secondary school system of England and Wales is about to be fundamentally restructured for the third time in forty or so years. This will involve a colossal expenditure of financial resources, the energy and talent of those who work in the schools and will, of course, be disruptive to the children. These periodic upheavals happen partly because people cannot agree what children are capable of, and therefore about the kind of schools they need.

We all know from personal experience that intelligence varies from one individual to another. However brilliant the teaching, not all children are capable of the same level of achievement. Our common sense also tells us that intelligence can take many forms. For example, Howard Gardner of the Harvard Graduate School of Education, in his book *Frames of Mind*, identifies six types: the linguistic, the musical, the logical, the spatial, the physical and the personal. He concludes that it is the balance of intelligence in each person which determines whether they become poets or plumbers, politicians or pianists or philosophers, designers or painters or bricklayers, athletes or actors or social workers or surgeons.[3]

Furthermore, we know that particular strains of ability sometimes seem to run in families, but we also recognise that environment has a huge effect on performance.

The argument in education is not about variations in the intelligence of children considered individual by individual, but about whether children can be sorted into *groups* for the purpose of educating them. As we have seen, Ellen Wilkinson, the post-war Education Minister, believed that there were three types of child, so there should be three types of school. Many of those who support comprehensive education believe that there are no types, only an infinite variety of children with infinite possibilities for development. The arrangements for secondary education envisaged in the 1988 Reform Act seem to signal at least a partial shift back to Ellen Wilkinson's analysis.

But what *do* our children achieve, what are they capable of achieving, and how do we know?

We know a great deal about what our children do achieve. Bodies such as the National Children's Bureau in London have carried out massive longitudinal studies. They have taken, for example, every child born in a particular week and followed them in great detail through their entire school lives.[4] The information from such studies has given us a pretty clear picture of some of the learning processes inside school, with particular reference to variations between social classes, the sexes, and racial groups.[5]

For example, most primary school teachers would take a professional pride in having treated every child alike. Yet despite very genuine professional efforts we know that in most schools, by the age of 7 children from poor homes will have fallen behind children from better-off families. There will be, on average, a gap of about a year in the reading age. By 11 that gap will have widened to about three years. At 16 the qualifications achieved by the different groups of children will vary considerably. A child of professional parents is *twelve times* more likely to go to university than a child whose parents work in manual occupations. Of course there are individual exceptions to this pattern: I am one myself. But the general pattern has been documented repeatedly.

Other currents can be identified in the river of children who flow through our schools. Once again, most teachers would try to treat boys and girls in a similar way, and to expect their results to be unaffected by gender. But there are large differences between how girls and boys, as groups, learn and behave. Of course there are individual exceptions: what we are observing is the majority.

What all the research evidence seems to tell us about girls is that they are a clever crowd: over and over again girls in primary schools have a higher mean score in mathematics and verbal reasoning tests than boys. According to ILEA figures that superiority of performance – slight but measurable – can still be detected at 16.[6] There is also a well documented difference between the subjects that girls and boys choose to study. The most recent figures I have seen showed that in English, French and Social Studies at A-level about three quarters of the students who entered the examinations were girls. In maths and physics, about three quarters were boys.[7]

Despite changes in the roles of women, it remains true that girls and boys have different aspirations. A recent survey of 600 children aged between 7 and 12 found that the girls wanted to be nurses, hairdressers, teachers or to work with children, while boys wanted to be engine drivers, pilots and so forth.[8]

If we move from class and gender to racial patterns we find that there are no national statistics on how children from the ethnic minorities fare in schools. In 1986 the House of Commons Home Affairs Subcommittee on Race Relations and Immigration called for such statistics to be collected: 'Without them little idea can be gained of the degree and nature of disadvantage faced by particular communities.'[9] The Committee had to rely on information gathered by ILEA, which in 1985 had looked at the examination results of African, Asian, Arab, Bangladeshi, Caribbean English, Scottish, Welsh, Irish, Greek, Indian, Pakistani, South East Asian, and Turkish children.[10]

There seemed no particular reason why the different groups of children should perform differently in verbal reasoning tests and examinations, but in fact quite clear distinctions emerged. Bangladeshi, Turkish and Afro-Caribbean children's results were below average in the two years studied.

There is little real disagreement about the fact that children, as groups, do tend to follow some rather similar and predictable tracks in school. The question is *why* these patterns exist, and what educational conclusions should be drawn from them.

Some people have argued that the fact that children from poor homes tend to fall behind in their reading progress so early in primary school tells us something very simple and obvious: namely that working-class people are innately less intelligent than middle-class people. The second Black Paper, for example, states: 'For generation after generation going well back before the days of the legendary Dick Whittington there has been an appreciable amount of social mobility. Bright children from the poorer classes forge their way upward and duller children from the higher classes drift downward. Class differences become inevitable in any civilised society.'[11]

Others, including myself, have argued that variations between the levels of achievement of children from different social backgrounds are in fact the consequence of environmental factors rather than of innate intelligence.

Which is right? It is a vital question, because the way in which the Government of the day has seen the answer to this question has determined the kind of schooling available.

Put simply, if working-class children are, as a group, less intelligent than middle-class children, why not provide a separate education in the straightforward skills needed for everyday life, along the lines of the old elementary school? If girls are born with a predisposition towards French, English literature and music, why not put them in separate schools and teach them those things? If middle-class boys are particularly good at maths and physics and the nation needs mathematicians and physicists, why not equip very good schools to help the boys develop their skills? This sort of thinking was in fact the basis of the education system of this country in the nineteenth century and for much of the twentieth.

What real evidence is there to support the theory that innate ability is determined by class, gender or race? In the nineteenth century, scientists measured the brain cavities of vast numbers of human skulls, and 'proved' that everything they had always believed was true. Men had bigger brains than women. White people had bigger brains than black people. Best of all, German scientists managed to 'prove' that German brains were bigger than French brains.

Modern scientists have reanalysed the records of their investigations. Rather like the local authority examiners who believed that boys and girls were of equal ability even if the figures didn't show it, the scientists cooked the books: they simply ignored the data that didn't fit. When the omitted data were included in the analysis their thesis fell apart.

The issue of innate ability is in fact a complicated one, hinging on the biological study of genes and chromosomes. It is very fully set out in *The Mismeasure of Man* by Stephen Jay Gould, who, after a full study of the evidence, concludes that there is really no scientific foundation for believing in the innate ability of groups.[12]

Harvey Goldstein, a professor at the Institute of Education in London and an eminent statistician, sums it up by saying: 'the variation between individuals within any group is almost as great as the variation between all the individuals on the planet'.[13]

At this point, of course, the pragmatic British thinker snorts with exasperation. Genes! Chromosomes! What has this to do with anything? Pupils should all be given the same test, and on the basis of the results be allocated to an appropriate school. Perfectly fair!

Unfortunately, we do not know *how* to test children fairly for that purpose. We do know, for example, that working-class children learn more slowly in primary school; any test will tell us that. What it will not do is tell us what those children have the *potential* to achieve.

Whatever method of organisation is adopted for the education service, it would benefit from accurate information on the performance and potential attainment of children, based on some kind of systematic monitoring. Indeed, educationists have been trying to devise a fair test for years.

The 11+ examination devised by Cyril Burt of the London County Council was supposedly a scientific test of intelligence. It has been discredited for a number of reasons. Intelligence is not a static quality: it can increase; it can be learned. Burt's test concentrated on only one kind of intelligence, the logical, identifying people skilled in handling long chains of reasoning. Furthermore, it quite obviously failed to identify the talented children it claimed to. Alan Walters, for example, economic adviser to Mrs Thatcher, failed his 11+. Not only did he fail the exam, he failed in arithmetic. Yet years later, as a statistics student, he came first of the thousands of candidates who sat the London BSc (Econ) exam in 1951.

In addition, the examination itself lost credibility. Cyril Burt's biographer L. S. Hearnshaw has suggested that he falsified figures to make it appear that his system was working when he knew it was not.[14]

In 1976 Prime Minister James Callaghan asked in a speech at Ruskin College: 'What is the proper way of monitoring the use of resources in order to maintain a proper national standard of performance?' He asked an expert body, the Assessment of Performance Unit, to examine the problem. More than ten years later, we still do not know how to find out what children are capable of attaining.

Currently Margaret Thatcher and Kenneth Baker are determined to test all children three or four times during their school lives: they too have yet to put forward a test that will do more than give us a general indication of the social class of the child.

If we cannot prove innate intelligence or potential, perhaps we can identify other factors which affect levels of performance. Is the cultural conditioning of the child's early environment the key?

We know that by the time children come to school at the age of 5 they have already learned, or failed to learn, a great deal, and that that early learning makes a difference to the pace, quality and type of learning they do at school. Children from low-income families, with poor housing, diet and health care, are at a disadvantage even before their formal education begins.

The facts that a very large proportion of Afro-

Caribbeans and Bangladeshis work in manual occupations, and that the West Indian community has a very
high proportion of single-parent families, have been suggested as comparable factors to those affecting the performance of working-class children.

Many detailed studies have been made about the images
girls absorb about themselves, and about boys, from television, their families and books compared to those boys
have even before their first day at primary school.[15] One
major investigation concludes: 'Working class girls have
the shortest educational careers. Their strong orientation
to early marriage is confirmed in a number of studies . . .
Working class boys are perhaps best represented in research literature . . . the sons of semi skilled and unskilled
manual workers (had) limited educational ambitions . . .
related to their choosing and obtaining jobs similar to their
respected fathers.'

The purpose of education for many middle-class girls is
to improve their marriage prospects. Others have professional ambitions. 'Middle class boys have the most
extended of educational careers since . . . the competition
for university places and for professional occupations is
now subject to closure by certification rather than
money.'[16]

Other cultural factors may affect achievement. For example, middle-class pupils have the advantage of speaking
the same middle-class English as their teachers. The sheer
stress for many working-class children of moving into the
educational world is difficult to convey. I still regard
middle-class English almost as a foreign language in which
I am word-perfect but not comfortable. I once tried to
convey the process to my colleague in Whitehall, Francis
Cripps, a brilliant economist, who had been to Eton. I
asked him to imagine that he had to learn to speak with,
say, a pronounced Yorkshire accent. Not only that, he had
to acquire the style and manners of working-class York-
shiremen such as my father so well that he would pass

unnoticed in their company. Then, and only then, could he study and express his ideas about economics. Such a notion is ridiculous, yet it is the process that I and many others have been through in reverse. Worse difficulties face those speaking English as a second language, and Creole speakers whose language varies from standard English yet is an important feature of cultural identity. The experience of racial discrimination in the community, offering pre-school pupils what the Rampton Report describes as 'stereotyped, negative or patronising views of their abilities and potential',[17] has been extensively documented.

Teachers themselves may, consciously or unconsciously, share the cultural conditioning which children have experienced, and this may result in them treating children differently.

All these tendencies are revealed both in professional experience and in scholarly studies. What effect they have we do not know. But it is clear that early environment makes a huge contribution to children's performance. Standard mass testing of all children at 7, 11 and 14 will reveal little about intelligence, progress or potential, or even how well or badly a school is doing. 'The abstraction of intelligence as a single entity, its location within the brain, its quantification as one number for each individual and the use of these numbers to rank people in a single series of worthiness invariably find that oppressed and disadvantaged groups, races, classes or sexes are inferior and deserve their status.'[18] The Black Paper writers argued from an entirely unsupported position that the intelligence of groups was innate. There is no basis for the view that the children of the wealthy are on average the most intelligent, destined to do best academically. Nor does it follow that the maximising of their capacities by the provision of exceptionally well funded schools, with highly trained teachers and privileged access to the best resourced and staffed universities in the country is the most rational use of society's resources.

No groups should be destined by birth to be 'hewers of wood and drawers of water', needing to be educated separately in the basic skills that they will need for the humble role they are destined to play in society.

Girls are not innately predisposed to artistic and domestic pursuits. The lower level of science and technical facilities in girls' schools, and of access to computer facilities even in mixed schools, is not a reflection of unchangeable reality. There are no scientific data to suggest that the lower number of boys who choose to study languages at 14 reflects an inherent masculine inability to be successful linguists, balanced by pronounced masculine abilities in nuclear physics. Scholastic performance of different ethnic groups is broadly predictable, but it does not follow that nothing can be done to change it.

What we must do is develop a system which does not simply accept, but aims to overcome the handicaps which affect the performance of each group or individual child.

SIX

The 'Crisis' in Our Schools

If the first essential flaw in Kenneth Baker's proposals is that they are based on a false premise about intelligence and groups, the second equally serious obstacle to their success is that most of the problems relating to schools themselves have been wrongly identified.

'Many of Britain's schools are in a state of crisis,' say Cox, Douglas-Home, Martin, Norcross and Scruton in 'Whose Schools? A Radical Manifesto', issued in December 1986. This document is the latest in a series of critiques of public education which began with the first Black Paper.

According to the Manifesto, standards had fallen since the beginning of this century. Primary schools were no longer teaching pupils to read and add up. Grammar schools were better educational institutions than comprehensive schools, which sacrificed the potential for achievement of the able child while failing to teach the less able child the elementary life skills necessary to find work. Mixed ability teaching was widespread and reinforced the inadequate teaching of the able child. 'Producer capture', the tendency of the public planning institutions to act in the interests of those who worked in the service at the expense of those who used it, was to blame.

The egalitarian dislike of tests and examinations, presented as a desire to protect the children from failure, was in reality a device to disguise low standards and poor performance by the professionals.

These are some of the main problems which the critics

identify and which the reforms in educational administration are designed to solve. Is their analysis true?

In my opinion it is almost impossible to say anything
sensible on the question of whether standards have fallen
or risen at any time compared with any other time. As
Caroline St John Brooks pointed out in *New Society*: 'In
1920, fewer than one in three of the country's 14 to 15 year
olds were in school at all. A quarter were in elementary
schools and 8 per cent were in secondary schools which
educated the School Certificate candidates.'[1] Transfer
from elementary school to secondary school was not easy;
in 1919–20 fewer than 1 per cent actually made the
change.

The number of pupils who emerged from school with a
qualification School Certificate, was tiny – 4 per cent of the
16–17 age group. In contrast, by 1982 over 25 per cent of
all school leavers had five or more O-level passes, while 20
per cent were achieving an average C grade in seven or
more subjects. This was despite the fact that Ellen Wilkinson, when Education Minister in the 1940s, had set the
GCE O-level pass mark high because she wanted to prevent
the new secondary modern schools from entering pupils
for it.

The original evidence for the proposition that standards
had fallen came from Cyril Burt, the architect of the 11+
examination. His original article in the *Irish Journal of
Education*, later reproduced in the Black Papers, set out
evidence said to be based on a table of scores for intelligence and school attainment compiled by a Miss M. G.
O'Connor from various reports from 1914 to 1965. The
years 1914, 1917, 1920, 1945, 1955 and 1965 were cited,
and the level reached in each of the three Rs was shown to
have declined significantly since 1914. Average intelligence also showed a slight decline.

Burt's biographer, L. S. Hearnshaw, has examined this
evidence and suggests it is fraudulent. Certainly Burt was
involved in testing children in 1914, and he commented at

that time: 'Pedagogical tests are in urgent need of standardisation. The results of examination at present conducted are notoriously unscientific.' However, Hearnshaw continues: 'It is clear that Burt was not in a position to provide reliable norms for school achievements in 1914. The tests he was later to use had not at that time been standardised nor if they existed been employed on any but small pilot groups.'[2] Thus Burt could not give the achievement levels for 1914 with any authority, yet these levels are used as a standard for comparison.

The figures for 1955 and 1965 are even more mysterious. After investigating the records of the LCC and Burt's diaries and correspondence, Hearnshaw writes: 'It seems improbable in the extreme that any testing programme was carried out under Burt's direction either in 1955 or 1965 ... there are other difficulties ... Burt had no research funds at his disposal and a programme that involved hundreds of hours of testing ... must have been expensive to mount ... finally there is no evidence of contact or communication with Miss O'Connor.'[3]

What about the increase in the percentage of children taking and passing O-levels? Does that mean that standards at any given period have risen? Again, it is difficult to say.

Public examinations like these were 'norm referenced', which simply means that the examiners decided in advance the percentage of children who would pass, and maintained it year by year. Add to that the fact that there are a number of examining boards, each of whom have different syllabuses and marking schemes for the same subjects, and it is obviously difficult to draw any conclusions from comparing examination results. Now that the GCE/CSE system has been changed to the GCSE, we have reached a point where nobody can confidently comment on the basis of examination data. As the parent of a child who has just passed through the GCSE course my personal experience tells me that children cannot have been asked to do much more even in the legendary days of 1912.

Government Inspectors provide the best evidence we have. Their survey of 185 maintained and voluntary schools between 1982 and 1986 in 80 of the 97 local education authorities in England found that three quarters of the schools inspected were performing satisfactorily or better, while one quarter were less than satisfactory. They concluded that there was no evidence to support the view that secondary schools were in a state of crisis or rapid decline.[4]

What of the crisis in the primary schools? Is it true that children are no longer being taught to read and write? Apparently not. Once again, Government Inspectors who actually visited 1127 classes in 542 schools between 1975 and 1977 did not find this to be true.[5] Far from finding pupils doing whatever they liked, with reading, writing and arithmetic having been abandoned, they found what looked suspiciously like the old elementary school curriculum with the old elementary school teaching methods. In fact their criticism was that too much time was being spent on reading, writing and arithmetic exercises which were unrelated to anything else.

Another assessment, known as the Oracle Project, looked at what was happening in a sample of classrooms between 1975 and 1980. This university-based research confirmed the observations of HMI. The so-called revolution in primary schools which, it was suggested, was undermining standards and producing badly-educated students was a myth. Very little had changed.[6]

Much of the attack on poor standards focused on the comprehensive schools of England and Wales. There has never, of course, been a comprehensive *system* of secondary education. Instead there are schools with 'a wide variety of intake profiles due partly to creaming, but also to inequitable distribution between competing comprehensive schools due to the nature of some catchment areas, parental choice, selective entry and the varying calibre of feeder primary schools,' according to Alan Weeks in *Comprehensive Schools* (1986).[7]

In other words, because of the extensive private sector, the Government's Assisted Places Scheme and the effect of parental choice, many so-called comprehensives are similar in ability profiles to the old secondary moderns. Schools run by the church and other voluntary bodies may have more able children than other schools in their area.

Comparing school examination results in these circumstances is obviously difficult. How the comprehensive schools performed in relation to grammar schools is not known, because at the time that it could have been found out no one wanted to know. The Government did not commission appropriate comparative research. Weeks comments: 'On the first question of whether comprehensive schools would produce more meritocratic talent than tripartite schools, controlled longitudinal research was necessary . . . [it] would have cost a great deal of money, but not in terms of the national education budget . . . one gets the distinct impression that politicians were ill-disposed towards effective research fearful that the investigation would show the effectiveness of comprehensive schools or vice versa.' Of course the egalitarian principles that lie behind support for comprehensive schools aim at much more than examination results and jobs, but 'comprehensive schools have to achieve good meritocratic results, and then because of all the other benefits attributed to them they must achieve much more'.

In Scotland a fully comprehensive system of secondary education was established, and the effect on standards of attainment vigorously monitored by the Centre for Educational Sociology (CES) at Edinburgh University.[8] The results are examined in some detail later, but essentially the authors of the study found that children of all social groups improved their levels of achievement.

The critics' picture of mixed ability teaching is also

over-simplified. Firstly it was not widespread. The HMI survey of 10 per cent of all secondary schools between 1975 and 1978 found that mixed ability in most subjects existed in only 35 per cent of the first year of comprehensives, 23 per cent in years 1 and 2, 11 per cent in the first three years and 2 per cent in all five years.[9]

A study of London comprehensive schools showed that the most consistent pattern was 'a mixture of setting and mixed ability grouping in years 1 to 3 followed by a move to setting on its own in years 4 and 5'.[10] About half the schools followed this pattern.

Secondly, mixed ability teaching did not lead to lower standards. Studies of the effects of mixed ability teaching early in the secondary school seem to indicate that high ability pupils did *not* suffer, while lower ability pupils did better at O-level and CSE. HMI's criticism of the effect of mixed ability groupings on modern languages and science concentrated on the quality of the teaching rather than the system itself, while the National Foundation for Educational Research study concentrated on inadequate training and resourcing.

The issue of mixed ability grouping has been combined with that of ill discipline. To readers of the memoirs of public schoolboys the suggestion that school life in a State day school is not appropriately supervised is surprising. However, the issue is important and worth examining. In 1984 Martyn Denscombe surveyed all the available evidence and mounted a specific investigation. He concluded: 'Critics of standards of pupil behaviour in comprehensive schools have not generally based their allegations on substantial fact and . . . there are two good reasons for this. First there have been surprisingly few attempts at rigorous investigation and second there are inherent difficulties in measuring control problems.'[11] In his opinion there is no factual basis for the idea of a crisis of control in comprehensive schools. This view is supported by the Government Inspectors' 1987 report, which found that pupil behaviour in State schools was extremely good. Substantial pupil control difficulties were experienced in only 5 per cent of schools.

If the analysis of the weaknesses of State education put forward by the Black Paper writers was incorrect, does that mean that concern about standards and about the quality of education being received by children was misplaced?

Not at all. Faults had developed in the schools over and above those directly attributable to the Government disinvestment programme, but the Black Paper writers were unable to see them. Driven by a desire to prove the case for the replacement of a comprehensive *system* of secondary education with a segregated system based on selection tests at 11+ they argued, as they were bound to, that the system was failing. In reality the fault lay not with the system but with the variations in performance of schools within it, and of groups of schools in particular geographical areas.

For example, two very similar primary schools with parallel groups of children might be employing very similar teaching methods and devoting similar amounts of time to teaching reading, yet one school would achieve significantly better results than the other. Local authorities had not developed techniques for identifying schools that had fallen behind and bringing them up to standard.

There was, in other words, a crisis of management of the system, a crisis which was capable of a management solution but which would remain unaffected by changing the system, and might even be made worse.

Of course the Black Paper writers put forward a powerful critique of public management too, in the form of their analysis of 'producer capture' of the system. Here again their ideological goals caused them to carry their potentially powerful and relevant arguments to an illogical conclusion.

It was argued that the 'producers' of education – the teachers, lecturers, administrators and inspectors – ran the system. In addition, they alone assessed the quality of their own performance and had been excessively indulgent about their failures and extravagance. The producers had been supported by their trade unions, and by their councillor employers. Together they had formed local corporate conspiracies against the interests of parents, pupils and voters, conspiracies made possible because of the antiquated rating system which weakened local democracy.

A complete shift of power within education from local authorities to schools run by elected parent governors, freedom of information, competition and a poll tax paid by every adult would provide the antidote. The quality of education in our schools would be improved by making the producers accountable to the consumers – parents – who have the biggest stake in education, and create the efficient management of public resources because of the accountability of local councillors to every adult who was paying the poll tax.

The Black Paper writers, mostly academics, wrote and spoke as if theirs was the only criticism of public management being made. In fact during this period a transformation from within was slowly beginning in local government itself. The Audit Commission Handbook identifies two strategic eras. During the first, from 1945 to 1975, local management was geared to increasing spending in response to rising needs and expectations. From 1975/76, partly because of the limitations on spending, the beginning of a new strategic era could be detected (see Table 5).

A very gradual shift of emphasis away from centralised bureaucratic management towards central direction and decentralised management was one feature of the change. In arguing for a transfer of administrative responsibility to the schools, the education critics were thinking in parallel with some of the very councillors and planners with whom they politically disagreed. That transfer of responsibility

86   CHILDREN OF THE FUTURE

Table 5: Two Eras of Local Government Strategy

	1945–75 MEETING RISING EXPECTATIONS	1975– ADJUSTING TO AN ERA OF LIMITS
STRATEGY	Growth 'Bigger is better'	Redeployment 'Small is beautiful'
STRUCTURE	Fragmented Service/committee based	Central direction Delegated management responsibility
KEY SYSTEMS	Allocation of extra resources Control over inputs	Strategic Planning, Control Information on outputs, results
KEY SKILLS	Professional	General Management Political Technical (Information technology)
STYLE	Bureaucratic Risk averse	Managerial Experimental, innovative Participative
STAFF	Heavy central overhead Limited use of 'technology' Low pay/low productivity	Lean central overheads Intensive use of cost-saving 'technology' Average pay/'competitive' productivity

Source: Audit Commission Handbook, 'Improving Economy, Efficiency and Effectiveness'

was in tune with the times. Parents themselves argued for their greater involvement in the planning and organisation of the schools. Many felt great frustration at having to deal with slow-moving public bureaucracies. The door to the office of the Leader of ILEA in County Hall is blank, apart from the room number. Legend has it that the sign that used to be fixed to the door was removed by officials during the time of my distinguished predecessor Sir Ashley Bramall, after parents staged a prolonged sit-in in his room. The parents had been protesting because there were no places for their children at the schools to which they wanted to send them. I always used to wonder whether that anonymous panelled door to my room represented the protectiveness of officials towards the Leader, a back-handed bureaucratic tribute to the passion that parents feel about their children's schooling, or a statement that the real decision-maker was the Education Officer, and that all exciting events should take place in his room. As a result of the 1988 Act such activities should no longer be necessary.

The proposition that parent representatives with teacher representatives, should play a major role in running schools is a democratic one. In a healthy society as much power as possible should be exercised from below by voters and citizens acting individually or together, not by bureaucracies and managements. The burden of principle lies with the critics of the system, and in my opinion experience supports it too. Certainly the attack on public authority management carried weight. Bureaucracies become conservative institutions psychologically wedded to past practice. I recall, in January 1977, spending a month in a little room on the first floor of the Department of Energy reading through archive material on policy formulation, in order to prepare a review of energy policy for the Secretary of State. I came across the records of the TUC's submission on fuel policy in the late 1920s. To my surprise it was exactly the same as that supported by the TUC in 1977. Going through the records it was obvious that in times of labour shortage and union power, the TUC always demanded that energy policy should be planned by a body composed of equal numbers of employer and worker representatives, plus Departmental officials, and that the body should have an independent secretariat.

The Departmental bureaucracy always conceded the planning institution but refused the independent secretariat. That function they insisted on retaining for themselves. When jobs became scarce and the unions weaker the Department then withdrew its support for the planning body. This stately dance between the rival mandarin classes of government and organised labour had obviously less to do with successful energy planning than with the aspirations to power amongst the mandarins themselves. In my experience it is almost always true that administrative groups responsible for public planning work closely with the politicians, managements and trade unions in the field and become unreasonably and unreasoningly loyal to their own past plans. All tend to present what are in fact their own interests as if they were statements of the highest ethical principle, arrived at solely out of a concern for the greatest good of the greatest number. This may be only human, but it is not desirable.

The world of education seemed very similar to me when I arrived at the Inner London Education Authority in 1981. Leading elected members, Education Officers and trade union representatives worked closely together both informally and publicly on the committees of the Authority. Parents were involved at an outer sphere of decision making. The Authority kept secret the figures which would have enabled comparisons to be made between schools based on performance in examinations, the number of teachers actually working in the school and the number of teachers each school was entitled to.

While the annual budget received months of detailed attention by all members, the monitoring of the quality of education on a systematic, professional basis was a very recent development. Increasing expenditure was more important to most Labour members than improving quality. This was, I believe, true throughout most of the public education system. The consequences were a reluctance to close schools even when falling rolls meant it was in the interests of children to do so, and a reluctance to monitor the quality of education being provided by schools.

At ILEA, the responsibility for this lay with Labour members who formed the majority party: eventually their attitude changed and the information about schools was published. Elected parent representatives served on every school governing body. I successfully recommended that they should also become members, with votes on the decision-making committees of the Authority itself, alongside the elected members and teacher representatives. With the support of Ruth Gee, then Deputy Leader, Steve Bundred, Chair of Finance and Chief Whip Leslie Hammond, the information on the relative achievement of schools was published. During the years that it had been withheld, parents had been denied information they had a right to know about schools, and the policy-making of the Authority was damaged. The process of identifying and eliminating variations in the performance of schools was undoubtedly held back by that lack of openness. The many local education authorities which did not have the facilities to collect and prepare such information had even more difficulty in developing a programme to raise standards.

The case for a rationalisation of the relationship between local education authorities and schools was well made. No parallel justification has been advanced for the virtual destruction of the planning role of the local authorities. The vision of over 27,000 schools strategically managed by central Government has little to recommend itself over a reformed partnership between central and local government.

Why did the restructuring of the management of public education need to be so drastic, and so different from the local government pattern outlined in the Audit Commission's second strategic era?

In my opinion the reactionary writers who levelled the criticism of producer capture at local authorities were unwilling to follow that criticism through to its logical conclusion. They were opportunistic rather than principled. The criticism of producer capture, or corporatism as I would term it, depends for its moral and practical force on an implicit model of how public institutions ought to behave. That model assumes that a public body should adopt and declare clear goals and be prepared to override powerful sectional forces within the community. A duty of openness and preparedness to accept scrutiny by the press and critics is a part of that institutional model, which is the true converse of producer capture.

Ministers who support this critique of local government ignore its implications at national level. They believe, or at least claim to believe, in what they call market forces, which are in reality the results of decisions reached by private sector managements – producers, in other words. They and their supporters argue that Government must interfere as little as possible with these private sector producers. The known tendencies of these producers to fix prices, form cartels, sell goods and services to the public that vary from the unreliable to the positively dangerous, pollute the environment and to act in a manner inconsistent with the interests of citizens is barely acknowledged. Ministers by their inaction practise another form of producer capture nationally.

The proposal that local schools should emulate their model of the commercial market is open to the same criticism. Governors, responsible together with the head and teaching staff for 'selling' their schools locally, may simply create a system of small corporate conspiracies. They will naturally seek to conceal their failings and exaggerate their strengths. Those who do this with the help of marketing professionals will no doubt do it best. The governors in each school will be dependent for advice on the professionals in the school, who will be more, not less, powerful than before. The best-organised schools will fight ruthlessly for scarce resources irrespective of the true priorities in the area, and will thus distort the reshaped capital programme.

To sum up, the crisis which the Black Paper writers describe never took place. Their educational analysis was distorted by their desire to prove the case for selective secondary education. Their management critique, though powerful, was weakened by the disingenuousness of their case for market forces. The effect of their intervention was to distract attention from what was really wrong and to prevent the action that really needed to be taken to put it right.

SEVEN

The Vacuum at the Centre

In the early 1970s I accompanied Jack Straw, then President of the National Union of Students, on a memorable visit to the Department of Education and Science. In the course of the meeting a question was put to us by Toby Weaver, then deputy to the Department's Permanent Secretary.

'What is education for?' he asked. We were silent. Even Jack, who is normally good for a polished comeback, did not speak.

'Don't you know?' I asked.

'Not really,' said Toby Weaver suavely. 'We thought you would. After all, you're younger.'

Of course we were being teased. Top civil servants cannot avoid being struck by the contrast between their own pinstriped and self-disciplined style and the dishevelled muddle of some of the delegations they meet. Little jokes like this help relieve the tension caused by the contrast.

But this particular mandarin jest contained a kernel of truth. Successive Governments, while happy to make broad statements about the basis of the education they approve of, have been vague and indecisive about strategic goals. This vacuum at the centre was in my opinion the most important single cause of the problems in the education service.

For twenty years the Black Paper writers have been attacking the record of teachers, teaching unions, local authority administration and Labour councillors. They have every right to do so, but in the process they have distorted the agenda of national debate by deflecting it away from the Government.

If I were appearing before history's tribunal on behalf of those who worked in and administered the public education service, I would, while conceding that errors had been made by my clients, feel bound to enquire what the Government had been doing in the half-century or so since the locally administered national service had been set up. Government, after all, is enormously powerful. Despite Mrs Thatcher's references to rolling back the frontiers of the State, this power has increased rather than diminished so far as education is concerned. Ministers decide the framework of education by legislation and regulation. For years they have decided on local investment. They have agreed proposals for building schools, closing them down and reorganising them. They have decided the kind of public examinations that will be set, the number of teachers to be trained and the type of training, the number of places to be available in higher education. They monitor the service through their own Inspectorate. Despite these enormous powers, most Education Ministers have affected not to be in charge.

Sir Keith Joseph, when Secretary of State, appeared as an anguished seeker after truth in an almost impossibly complex and bewildering universe. Shirley Williams and James Callaghan launched a Great Debate and asked everyone else what to do.

'The Labour movement has always cherished education: free education, comprehensive education, adult education, education for life,' said Callaghan, then Prime Minister, at Ruskin College in October 1976. He continued: 'The fields that need study because they cause concern . . . are the methods and aims of informal instruction, the strong case for the so-called core curriculum of basic knowledge . . . what is the proper way of monitoring the use of resources in order to maintain a proper national performance, the role of the Inspectorate in relation to national standards . . . and the need to improve relations between industry and education?'

Kenneth Baker has gone further. He has repealed the duty laid upon the Minister in the 1944 Act to present an annual report to Parliament.

The contrast with other Government Departments is quite marked. We know after all that the overriding strategic goal of economic policy is the control of inflation, and that other policies, however desirable, that conflict with that goal (such as full employment) will be sacrificed. It is really rather hard to imagine a post-war Chancellor expressing the public confusion that Education Ministers have. Indeed, Chancellors usually pretend to be more in charge than they actually are.

This is quite inconsistent with best practice in local government and the private sector. 'Any successful organisation, especially one involving political choice and action affecting the general public, requires some guiding concept,' says the Audit Commission Handbook. It needs a *vision* of what it is trying to achieve, and a *strategy* for translating this into reality. The *structure* of the service – the way it is organised to implement the strategy, and the *systems*, of planning, controlling and monitoring, are equally necessary. The critical resource in any public service is *people*. A plan for remitting training, motivating and rewarding is central to success, as is the intangible notion of *style* – the way we do things, the way Ministers relate to local authorities, to teacher representatives and to those they are there to serve.

To take another example: for many years the goal of energy policy enshrined in Acts of Parliament was the supplying of the energy needs of the nation at the lowest possible cost consistent with security of supply. This policy set very clear limits within which the planners had to work and by which their efforts could be curbed: it prohibited subsidising prices so that everyone could afford the cost of energy.

What then should be the key aims and objectives of education policy? The statutes are silent. Legislation cannot answer Toby Weaver's question, since the 1944 Education Act does not contain a description of the goals the education service is required to reach and by which its efforts can therefore be measured.

Perhaps we might ask instead the slightly simpler question of what purpose schools are meant to serve. One goal of a schooling system, presumably, is to inspire and educate children to express their abilities to the full. Such a goal throws into relief the serious mismanagement that has existed at national level, and still exists. There are five strategic problems.

Firstly, what is the minimum standard of physical provision to which every child is entitled in the Department's eyes, and how do we ensure that it is provided? Branches of the National Westminster Bank or Sainsburys or Marks & Spencer are more or less equally well built and well staffed wherever they are, and are continuously improved. That is not true of education. Secondly, the examination results of whole groups of schools vary widely according to their location. The Department knows of these variations because it publishes the annual chart which chronicles them. What action has Government taken to improve the schools in low-performing areas? What action should it take?

Even within a single geographical area, schools may vary in quality. Two schools containing similar numbers and types of pupils, equal numbers of teachers and similar facilities will produce different results. One public school may be more effective in educational terms than another of very similar staffing and intake. One custom-built comprehensive may be more effective than another apparently identical school two blocks away. This variation in the quality of similar schools was, until recently, neglected by many local authorities. What guidance should the Government give on this point? This is the third issue.

I can remember arguing passionately in the ILEA Schools Subcommittee that the most pressing need was for a tough and systematic programme of bringing less than adequate schools up to standard. For some reason, ILEA officers were unhappy with this approach. David Mallen, now Education Officer, and a person of great dedication and integrity, suddenly exclaimed: 'The truth is that there are schools in the Authority to which we would not send our own children.' He was later appointed as Chief Education Officer: he and Dr Hargreaves, the Chief Inspector, designed and began to implement precisely the programme that was so badly needed.

This issue, that the same types of school vary widely from each other, was established in a pioneering study led by Dr Peter Mortimer – the ILEA Junior School Project.[1] Published in 1986, the project is a longitudinal study of nearly 2,000 children from 7 to 11 years of age in fifty junior schools. The authors came to three major conclusions. Firstly, that there were marked differences between the schools in their effects on pupil progress. Secondly, the differences were substantial and affected all groups. Thirdly, that the variation was bound up with the management of the school.

A fourth question in need of a strategic response is that described clearly about twenty years ago in studies like the National Children's Bureau's 'From Birth to Seven' and Rutter's *Fifteen Thousand Hours*, namely that the early, pre-school years of a child have a very marked effect on the rate of progress of that child at school. Within each generation is a group who are literally born to fail but who, given the right educational environment, can overcome in varying degrees that early conditioning. What is to be done about this? Among Ministers, only Sir Keith Joseph when at the DHSS in the 1970s ever identified this as a possible goal.

A fifth question is the variation in the educational offers made to young people in this country beyond the age of 16 and those made in competitor economies in Western Europe. The number of young people undergoing training or higher education in Britain at the age of 18 is low in comparison with countries like Denmark, West Germany or France. At the same time a post-16 education and training programme which is not under the auspices of the Department of Education is developing, along lines inconsistent with the new national curriculum. An assessment of this strategic mismatch, and the quality of the post-16 offer, needs to be carried out.

Why has there been this neglect of strategy, and what has been the effect of its absence? The 1944 Act, by providing the structure that encouraged economic equality, assumed that the implicit goal of educational equality would follow of its own accord. A tradition developed of putting considerable effort into structure and buildings, but ignoring what happened inside them.

Reports such as Plowden, Newsom and Swann tackled aspects of this problem, but it has never been clear to what extent central Government, the commissioning agent, shared the views expressed in these Reports. An attempt was finally made by Keith Joseph in his March 1985 White Paper 'Better Schools'.[2] It stated: 'Government aims to raise standards at all levels of ability. To secure the best possible returns from resources that are invested in education.' It was never implemented.

Some might ask what effect, in day-to-day terms, clarity of Government thinking would have on what happens in schools. The answer is that without clear goals it is impossible for a Government Department to plan and assess its own role and for Parliament to hold the Executive to account.

Ministers have for example been notoriously badly informed about the effectiveness of State schooling and prone to take decisions and commit resources on ill-substantiated grounds. The most glaring instance is the creation of three different types of school for three different types of children, but there have been other blunders of equal seriousness.

The switch to comprehensive education was not accompanied by the detailed monitoring which was the only way that such a huge strategic alteration could have been fairly assessed. Controlled longitudinal research was needed. Unfortunately the only substantial, large-scale official research project said that it was impractical to compare comprehensive schools with any other kind of school.

The consequence of this was of course that research was done by pro- or anti-comprehensive school campaigners who engaged in a public war of statistics which reinforced the prejudices of those who had already made up their minds but offered little guidance to those who were not yet committed. According to R. Pedley: 'No deep research was done and it will never be known whether comprehensive schools [were] really better at the meritocratic game . . . perhaps it was impossible to discover even in the 1970s but that will never be known either.'[3]

The role of the Minister as puzzled philosopher fed through into a diminution of the role of the Schools Inspectorate. In 1922/23 the Board of Education's view was that its 368 Inspectors should visit every school in the land once a year and inspect it every three years. This three-yearly inspection was, of course, a pious hope.

By the 1950s few grammar schools were inspected more than once a decade, and by 1968 the head of HM Inspectorate could tell the House of Commons Select Committee that the aim of cyclical inspections had been abandoned in favour of 'better' ways of monitoring the service. 'Some schools,' his predecessor had observed, 'will never be inspected.' HM Inspectorate simply faded away as the guardians of the interests of the nation's children.

Government, badly informed and remote, was directly responsible for the muddle over curriculum and teaching method. Historically, the shaping force of the secondary school curriculum has been the 16+ examination (the so-called ordinary level examination). It was devised for 20 per cent of the school population, with the specific aim of selecting those who were to continue their school education until the age of 18 and go on to college or university. This need to provide for the choices made by only one fifth of the pupils shaped the timetables of all secondary school pupils up to the age of 16. In the mid sixties a further examination was added, the CSE, aimed at testing the abilities of a further 40 per cent of pupils, each making individual subject choices on the same model. The task of timetabling and planning, in the absence of a curriculum philosophy, became akin to developing a strategy for predicting the winning numbers at the roulette tables.

The curriculum choices made by examination candidates have resulted in individual timetables that have not reflected sound education practice – for example, girls as a group have tended to give up maths and sciences and boys languages. In 1977 the DES issued a Green Paper, 'Education in Schools, a consultative document', which suggested that Government should perhaps determine certain areas of the curriculum. A circular, 14/77, reminded LEAs that they had curricular responsibilities and asked what their policies were: it transpired that few had a policy for secondary schools. So far as primary education was concerned many, like the ILEA, had devolved responsibility to schools. 'A Framework for the School Curriculum', published in 1980, was seen as a somewhat shallow document.

It was left to Sir Keith's 1985 White Paper 'Better Schools' to admit that there was 'widespread acceptance of the view that broad agreement about the objectives and content of the school curriculum is necessary'. The document went on to explain that Government could not discharge its planning functions without a curriculum policy, and neither could the LEAs: 'The Secretaries of

State need a curricular policy for discharging their statutory duty . . . and their more specific duties for example in relation to their pattern of schools and supply and training of teachers.'

The failure of central Government to develop a curriculum philosophy led to a tradition that the school curriculum was a matter which fell within the professional competence of the teaching profession, and that it was an expert business in which only teachers should play any part in deciding either curriculum content or teaching method. This tradition grew out of the necessity for teacher self-reliance created by the vacuity of Government thinking in the 1940s.

Government publications of that period clearly specified that while the minority of children would follow the Morant plan of 1904, the majority were to learn by doing, in an environment which did not stress the three Rs, and the teachers in the schools were to work out what that meant.

The abdication of responsibility by Government and its acceptance by the teaching profession was subsequently institutionalised in the sixties by the establishment of the Schools Council for Curriculum and Examinations, in which teachers had a majority membership of important committees. The body failed, however, to develop a national policy for the curriculum. There was no place within the Schools Council for discussion about the whole curriculum, only for curriculum development in such a way that teachers could be assisted to improve their own curriculum planning and teaching methods.

The curriculum was always too important to leave to the teachers in each school: and there are common elements to all primary and secondary schools which need to be agreed on and established. That this took forty years to be realised is a comment on the amateur tradition of Government.

The motive for giving freedom to teachers to determine the curriculum has been justified as the expression of a nineteenth-century political tradition which emphasised the importance of restricting the level of State intervention in the content of education. John White (1975) cites the abolition of the Elementary School Regulation by the Conservative President of the Board of Education Lord Eustace Percy in 1926 as an earlier expression of this tradition.[4]

Such high-minded concern for the public good may be at the heart of the lack of guidance given to schools in the 1940s: alternatively, it may simply have been a patrician indifference to the educational needs of the 80 per cent of children in the secondary modern schools. There was, after all, a curriculum plan for the grammar schools.

The Whitehall explanation for this absence of strategic policy, monitoring and planning is lack of power. For years, officials of the Department of Education and Science have been lamenting their lack of direct administrative power over the schools.

Now all that has changed. Instead of trying to direct events through the building regulations, DES-appointed working groups are deciding on what children will actually be taught. They are sorting out when children will be examined and on what, and drafting directives on the phased introduction of the master plan. The Department of Education and Science has become a dirigiste Department, in a move which runs completely counter to the anti-State policies of Government. At the heart of this directive policy lies the new national curriculum and the accompanying system of testing. Kenneth Baker now seems to have a strategic plan. Is it the right one?

EIGHT

The Franchise Strategy

For decades, Ministers and civil servants have been poring over the plans of school buildings without having any clear idea of what should go inside them. This absurd era is now over.

There is a vision – partially undeclared – a strategy and a detailed educational plan. The national service, locally administered, is no more. Instead the Department of Education is managing the schools on a franchise system. What pupils are taught, and how they are tested, is to be laid down by Government. Which school the pupils attend, and how many are on the roll, is a matter for parental choice. The amount of money available from Government is contracting, and Ministers have provided for a number of schools to leave the system and form an alternative consortium, separately managed and presumably catering for a different class of customer.

The national curriculum is the cornerstone of the franchise system. How it can work when there is a shortage of teachers, books, equipment and adequate technical facilities is not clear. The plan, however, deserves to be examined in good faith, as it is a long-overdue reform. How will it help pupils within schools and when they leave to seek work? How does it relate to the huge programme of training being developed for post-16-year-olds?

The Education Reform Act requires the Secretary of State, LEAs, governing bodies and head teachers to secure a school curriculum which 'promotes the spiritual, moral, cultural, mental and physical development of pupils' and to 'prepare such pupils for the opportunities, responsibilities and experiences of adult life'. To fulfil these requirements, the Secretary of State has decided that there are to be three core subjects (English, mathematics and science) and seven foundation subjects (technology, history, geography, music, art, physical education and, for secondary schools only, a modern foreign language). Religious education, the only part of the curriculum laid down in the 1944 Act, is to be compulsory for all students including sixth-formers.

For each of these core and foundation subjects there will be a series of benchmarks. These will be a list of national attainment targets encompassing the understanding, knowledge and skills that each pupil must show in each subject at each of ten levels. These ten levels and the related national testing system are explored in Chapter 10.

To draw up these lists or benchmarks, the Secretary of State has appointed a number of task groups working to a National Curriculum Council. The members of the National Curriculum Council have been carefully selected, and there are rumours that some very respected and prominent educationalists have been interviewed and rejected because their views do not seem to accord with those of the Government. There have already been three reports from task groups looking into the benchmarks for maths, science and English, and reports will continue to come out over the next six to seven years.

LEAs, heads and governors will be legally obliged to see that the national curriculum is taught, and the advisory service of local education authorities will have to advise schools on the national curriculum and ensure that they are carrying it out. LEAs will have to set up a means by which complaints can be heard about the way schools are teaching the national curriculum and RE. If the local complaints machinery does not give satisfaction, an appeal can be made to the Secretary of State, who can overrule the complaints machinery.

Superficially, it looks as if the Government has done the right thing. It has noted the fatal flaw in the 1944 Education Act and devised a national curriculum. It appears that there will be, once again, a plan to put the heart back into education. For this action, the Government must be congratulated. However, just as the lack of curriculum direction in the 1944 Act was a fatal flaw, so the direction in which the national curriculum is now being steered may prove the fatal flaw in the 1988 Act. The idea of a subject curriculum and a series of attainment tests has an unhappy history. Its roots lie in the Revised Code of 1862 and the Inspectors who went around testing pupils between 1862 and 1895. If pupils failed to give the correct answers to the questions put to them by these Inspectors, the school did not receive its full monies from the public purse. This was the notorious 'payment by results' system. The thing to note here is not the organisation of the system, but the way in which the curriculum was defined by the questions that the Inspectors asked, supposedly based on the Revised Code. No one, reflecting on this period, can fail to be struck by the oddity and idiosyncrasy of a curriculum determined in this peculiar and unthinking way. It remains to be seen whether the task groups will be better than these notorious Inspectors.

There is a further historical parallel in the 1904 Regulations for Secondary Schools and the 1904 Code of Regulations for Public Elementary Schools. These regulations appear to stem from the concerns of the Royal Commission on Technical Instruction which drew attention to the paucity of schooling for future workers when it compared England with the Germany of 1884: 'The one point in which Germany is overwhelmingly superior to England is in schools, and in the education of all classes of the people. The dense ignorance so common among workmen in England is unknown.'[1] Secondary schools were to teach English language and literature, at least one language other than English, geography, history, mathematics, science, drawing, singing, manual instruction (boys), domestic subjects (girls), physical exercise and organised games. The curriculum for the elementary school was to contain English language, handwriting, arithmetic, drawing, practical instruction in handicraft, gardening, domestic and other subjects, observation lessons and nature study, geography, history, singing, hygiene, physical training and moral instruction. These regulations look surprisingly similar to the foundation and core subjects of today's national curriculum. The complaint that workers in other countries were better educated than those in England also has a contemporary ring. Interestingly, the regulations were abolished when it appeared that a Labour Government might be elected to power. The roots of the present national curriculum lie deep in the thinking of Victorian Britain, the age of industrialisation, poverty and deep schisms between the different classes of society. But is it wrong for that reason?

Partly the concern is that the national curriculum is based on a very traditional understanding of secondary education. Those who conceive of the curriculum as a list of subjects justify that list by stating that the subjects contain the core of a culture which should be passed on to future generations. The purity of the subject must not be diluted. Certain subjects which they believe to be important are being omitted from the curriculum, so they claim, and new subjects or areas of the curriculum are not 'proper' subjects.

Most of these critiques originate in a view that subjects are natural compartments of knowledge, and that there are a number of these subjects which have their own hierarchy. The apex of that hierarchy is almost invariably to be found in a university department, where the area of knowledge has been studied and pondered over for generations. There appears to be an unspoken argument that if what are considered the best minds have been working on the subject, that should be good enough for younger minds. A further part of the argument is that young minds must be prepared for the ultimate educational experience – 'reading' a particular subject at university. To prepare for this 'reading' pupils must have reached a certain standard in that subject. To ensure that the best minds are fed into the university system, there must be competition between students and only the best will be rewarded with a place in academia.

The argument that all worthwhile knowledge must be organised within subjects is superficially very attractive. It makes it easy for us to understand knowledge; it satisfies a desire for organisation and order. At present, society awards status to individuals on the basis of their achievement in a particular subject area, so we naturally hanker for success in a subject. Teachers are well versed in certain subjects and see their own future success, status and satisfaction in those subject terms. It is so ingrained in our culture that it is easy to understand a school curriculum described in terms of subjects. It even makes it easy to organise the training of teachers and to check that they have the appropriate knowledge. In the schools and the LEAs it makes administration far simpler. Everything can be tucked into tidy compartments. Finally, it makes it very easy to assess whether pupils have achieved a certain standard. They simply take an examination in a particular subject and either gain or fail to gain a certificate.

It is thus very easy to see why the Government finds it simpler to revert to formulae about the percentage of the curriculum that should be devoted to this or that subject. It pre-empts difficult thinking and even more difficult public debate. The Government gives the impression of being on the side of excellence and 'standards' and of promoting a common, unified view of society and its traditions and culture.

Just because something is easier and administratively more simple does not make it right. One only has to remember that there were debates spanning literally a hundred years before science was accepted as a subject worthy of being taught at a university. Economics suffered the same fate at the hands of academics. Few people would deny that computer literacy ought to be a part of the curriculum, yet this is a subject without a university base, and has been one of the success stories of our education system. The work of our schools in this field has become the envy of the world.

Knowledge is not in fact compartmentalised. It is packaged in subjects because it has to be organised somehow. There is nothing that says the packaging we have is the right one or even the most appropriate one for the world we now live in. Finally, our culture should be seen as dynamic rather than as a dusty idea from the past which has to be passed along in some kind of educational pass the parcel. Culture is not a package of subjects that previous generations have wrapped up for us. Cultures change and develop; they are always moving forward. That is what makes society so exciting and stimulating.

So, knowledge does not necessarily have to be bundled up into subjects and there is more to culture than receiving a compulsory eleven years' worth of subjects. This does not mean that subjects should be thrown out. What it does mean is that we should not necessarily accept a national curriculum that is composed of an allotment of subjects. It is as much about processes, attitudes, skills, co-operation, problem solving and the application of understanding as it is about simply learning facts.

Perhaps the greatest challenge lies in the last two or three years of the comprehensive school, for it is at this point that the most criticism, disappointment and disillusion is focused. This is not to denigrate the work of the nursery, primary or junior secondary school teachers, which is vital, but unless the last years of secondary education are right, it is difficult to give direction to what comes before. It is far better to look at the last years of compulsory education as the pivotal point of education than to try to build a system which sees university education as the fulcrum from which the direction of the school curriculum is determined.

What should – or could – a curriculum contain? There can be no argument about whether the curriculum should include literacy. But there is far more to expressing oneself than the written word. The spoken word is just as important, if not more important. After all, we give directions and instructions, hold arguments, put our point of view, make complaints and undertake enquiries through the spoken word more than through the written medium. Literacy needs to be put within the context of communication skills, which include all forms of communicating including telephone, computers and film and video. Communication must thus reflect the world we live in, not the ivory towers of academia where the emphasis is on essays and learned articles.

Equally there should be numeracy. Again we need to think carefully about what this means. Does it mean learning how to do certain kinds of sums irrespective of whether that kind of computation is ever going to be useful, or does it mean learning to apply mathematics to solve real problems? Should we learn like parrots or should the curriculum teach us to understand mathematical ideas so that we can develop new insights or ways of dealing with the world? Is mathematics a hierarchy of ideas, a mountain to climb in which only those who have crossed the foothills and started on the inclines can hope to reach the top, or is it a network of interlocking ideas? Does it mean only learning those aspects which are useful to industry, or is there more to numeracy than this? When a start is made on answering these questions, schools will be in a position to create a mathematical curriculum in the classroom; until then, schools are left open to every criticism because there are no criteria against which to judge them except rather facile comparisons with other countries.

The world has become a far more technical place. Computers and electronics play an ever greater part in our lives, a fact which should be reflected in the curriculum. But it is not enough simply to say that there should be technology in the curriculum and leave it at that. What does that mean to a teacher faced with twenty-five 14 or 15 year-olds? What does it mean to the community? Does it mean a new 'subject' like physics or does it mean the application of technology to solve problems? If the latter, there is a serious difficulty for assessment and examinations in their traditional form, for there does not appear to be a body of knowledge which counts as 'knowing technology'. Even if there is such a body of knowledge, no one has yet defined it. It may be that what is most important is the attitude to technology. Many generations have grown up despising or afraid of technology. To a society that understands it, technology presents a power to be harnessed, not a threat.

For far too long politics has been treated as a subject to be avoided in schools, yet our society is a democracy, in which every citizen should have the opportunity to participate. Participation, political judgement and an understanding of society involve skills and knowledge which young people should have. To deny them these smacks suspiciously of political manipulation. True, there is the issue of indoctrination to be faced, but it needs to be confronted openly and honestly. When everyone sees political, economic and social understanding as a natural part of education, the likelihood of any one person having undue influence is extremely remote. More to be feared in a democracy is the insidious indoctrination of ignorance.

Many people will be familiar with the idea of pastoral care in schools. Described in this way it sounds as if its purpose is keeping young people out of trouble. If, however, it is seen as guidance and counselling, providing the opportunity for pupils to see what they are doing, to set targets for themselves, and to negotiate parts of their curriculum, it becomes far more positive and dynamic, a contribution to self-knowledge and learning to control one's own life, not a means by which the school tries to control the individual. A curriculum which incorporates this will truly be *teaching* discipline, a far worthier aim than *imposing* it.

All students should have the opportunity for work experience on an employer's premises (often known as WEEP). WEEP is about experiencing work – the disciplines of the workplace, the need for certain kinds of skills, knowledge and understanding, and the kind of problems which have to be solved – rather than just experiencing the particular kind of work that takes place in the industry where the WEEP takes place. It is not merely about understanding the world of work, but also about students understanding their own reaction to the experience and learning from it and about broadening their understanding of the world at large.

It is regrettable that the creative arts, music, dance, painting, sculpture, and the range of creative crafts, which all involve 'doing', have been seen as poor relations to the so-called academic subjects. These expressive and creative activities are important areas of human experience and vital elements in a 'good' education. Not only do they make life more fulfilling, they also have practical everyday and work implications. Not only is there now more interest in do-it-yourself, but more and more industries are concerned to bring an aesthetic element to their work.

These are just some of the elements that are important in the curriculum. It is totally inadequate to simply list subjects or elements as if this created a curriculum plan. If we as a society take the education of our young people seriously, then we are under an obligation to take curriculum planning seriously. Anyone, be it Government or LEA, which tries to fob the community off with a list is either selling society short or has its own plans for society. So what is the alternative? Surely we should be slightly less concerned with the subjects themselves, and slightly more with the fostering of other skills and qualities. The ability to work as a member of a team, for instance, is vital in many aspects of adult life. Reliability, perseverance and sensitivity are also as important as an individual's academic record.

One important recent curriculum development is the London Compact, which I launched when at ILEA and which is modelled on an idea put into practice in Boston. Basically it is an agreement between the school community and the business community. Both partners to the agreement or 'compact' undertake to do certain things; the schools may agree to meet certain target achievements while the business community may undertake to provide work experience placements and a guarantee of a job interview for students meeting the targets.

The London Compact was able to move into its pilot phase far quicker than in the USA because we at ILEA were able to learn from their experience, and because members of the Authority, schools, and parents and governors recognised that what it was trying to do was educationally worthwhile. Equally important was the fact that ILEA had already entered into a discussion with the industrial community in London. These discussions had led to the formation of the London Education Business Partnership, a joint Agency (LENTA) involving ILEA and a consortium of major companies committed to the development of small businesses and urban renewal. This partnership was able to bring the educationalists and the businessmen together to forge agreements. Not only would this lead to an increased understanding of each other's role, it could also harness resources for initiatives in the interest of inner London and its residents. Although it is the London Compact which is of interest here, there are a number of other exciting developments also sponsored by the partnership.

It is important to look at what the London Compact, formally negotiated and agreed by the members of the

London Education Business Partnership on behalf of their respective organisations, involves in practice.

The plan is less concerned with the precise choice of subjects than the qualities they reveal and test. Dr Hargreaves, Chief Inspector of ILEA, specified four kinds of learning: the acquisition and use of information; the practical application of knowledge; personal and social skills including communications; and motivation, commitment and enterprise. The compact encompasses these different kinds of learning.

What is immediately apparent is that these targets can be monitored. Industry can see whether the schools are meeting their goals and schools can see whether industry is keeping its side of the bargain. There is an agreed basis which can be assessed; a compact which can be monitored.

This, however, is just the beginning. Schools are beginning to see the compact as not merely a limited agreement, but a vehicle for thinking about the curriculum; it is becoming a factor in the process of developing a curriculum plan in the school. It is also bringing the world of industry into the school; bringing the real problems that industry and commerce face and asking schools to help find solutions; suggesting curriculum examples; provoking schools into thinking about the skills and attitudes they foster; making industry think about the way it manages and motivates young people; bringing about an understanding of the subtle and complex processes of education in which teachers are engaged. Teachers and industrialists are exchanging roles and sharing their perspectives on each other's work. New resources are being brought into the curriculum of some inner London schools.

It is not an easy process. It requires planning, negotiation, commitment and resources. It requires, in short, the context of an LEA curriculum planning process. To envisage that this kind of development could take place without an LEA taking a local and strategic view of the curriculum is naive. It is possible that individual schools could make some progress, but to imagine that an individual school could negotiate a version of the London Compact would be laughable if it were not so tragic. Thus the London Compact shows the importance of local education authority planning and the restrictions that will be placed on the curriculum if this important level of management and planning is excluded.

Not only does the Government's new national curriculum embrace and enhance the conservatism of the Victorian era in an age of rapid change when flexibility is crucial, and not only does this national curriculum exclude many important skills, but it creates a framework which is totally incompatible with some of the most exciting and innovative developments that the Government itself has helped to introduce, and fails to address the needs of the tertiary sector.

In 1983 the Government announced a £10 million investment in what was termed the Technical and Vocational Education Initiative. This pilot scheme was to fund the development of a new practical, technically orientated, vocational adjunct to the academic bookishness of the secondary curriculum. The initiative was to be jointly announced by Lord Young on behalf of the Manpower Services Commission, which was to put up the money, and Sir Keith Joseph, then Secretary of State for Education. Almost symbolically Lord Young held the press conference announcing the scheme without his educational colleague.

Contrary to the myths now being created, the education profession did not reject the scheme. It was seen as an opportunity to find the funds to implement the kind of curriculum reforms that teachers had been longing for. The teaching professions asked for an immediate meeting to negotiate the criteria for the scheme. They met Geoffrey

Holland, Director of the Manpower Services Commission, within days. Sir Keith Joseph offered a meeting in three months' time. The overriding suspicion was that the Department of Education and Science wanted the teaching profession to reject the scheme. It had its own conservative agenda.

Within months over seventy LEAS had submitted schemes. Those which had not submitted did not necessarily oppose the TVEI. Some had their own plans and priorities already and did not wish them to be sidetracked. Others were suspicious that they would suddenly find themselves saddled with expensive pilot schemes which they could not replicate across all their schools. Still others were suspicious of the confusion of roles between the MSC and the DES. All applauded the underlying educational aims.

The amount of money available for TVEI grew, and now almost every LEA is involved. Like the London Compact, the TVEI spawned new thinking and educational processes. Like the London Compact, it is difficult to see how the TVEI can sit alongside the national curriculum. The aims, processes, skills and ways of working are not compatible with the hierarchical lists that the Secretary of State's task groups are drawing up. The national curriculum of hierarchical lists is totally compatible with the traditional sixth form. However, even in the heartlands of affluence, where parents aspire to the old-fashioned ideal of the lower and upper sixth, fewer than half of the fifth-year students will stay on in the school sector. More commonly only a third of the fifth year stay on.

What happens to all those thousands of students who do not go into the sixth? Quite unbeknown to the Department of Education and Science, it would appear, they are entering the alternative system of education and training which is being developed by the Training Agency (as the Manpower Services Commission is now known). They are entering the Youth Training Scheme, now a two-year scheme. The Youth Training Scheme (YTS) has developed to fill a void. On the one hand the DES had nothing to offer those who did not enter the sixth form, while on the other hand industry was not prepared to offer the levels of training found in Britain's economic competitors, although it was quite ready to complain that young people did not have the skills it required. The MSC, as it then was, attempted to provide the bridge from school to adult working life. It tried to provide the skills which would enable young people to find satisfaction in work and to meet the needs of business and industry. It is trying to find ways of providing a profile of achievement, not unlike the London Record of Achievement, for all young people on the scheme. This profile, it is hoped, will outline their abilities and help them find jobs. The whole curriculum which emphasises skills and learning through experience, not subjects, is completely removed from the rationale that underpins the national curriculum. Young people leaving school will move from one set of educational values, embodied in the national curriculum, to another, with no connection between. It is a strategic muddle.

Stretched like a fragile web between the traditional sixth form and the newly developing YTS system are the colleges of further education. The DES, in the early 1980s, made a careful examination of further education provision, and instead of coming up with a plan for its development merely opined that most of it was probably illegal! The colleges developed despite the DES and provide academic education, basic training and higher vocational skills.

However, the crisis in local government finance is slowly and inexorably putting such a strain on further education provision that it is doubtful if it will survive. After all, an LEA only has to fund further education minimally.

The implications of this are that the national curriculum is not national. It ignores the needs of over half of our post-16 students. It is totally oblivious to the fact that an education and training curriculum of gigantic proportions is developing alongside the traditional sixth form with quite different aims and objectives.

To anyone who considers the situation rationally, it is absurd. There should be a unified system of post-16 education and training – a tertiary sector – which provides for all; a system which enables young people to move from vocational training to academic study and back with ease and facility. Instead we have something worse than the old tripartite system. Young people are channelled into areas which do not allow access to higher education and higher training just as they were channelled into secondary modern schools at 11+. What is so incomprehensible is that the DES has failed to recognise that these channels exist!

What can be said about the national curriculum? It is potentially a very important development. Unless the Government has a plan for the curriculum, it only has half an educational plan. The quarrel is not with the idea of a national curriculum, it is with this Government's idea of what the national curriculum should be. The curriculum has been couched in the language of academic subjects. It does not take into account all the skills and attributes which should be considered. It is rigid and inflexible without a proper mechanism which will allow it to develop and grow. It provides a minimal framework which will restrict and become the maximum. It is the creation of a narrow clique and fails to engage the whole community. It ignores exciting innovations such as the London Compact and TVEI. Finally, it fails to address the tertiary sector. What are its implications for the personal education of young people, their preparation for adulthood?

NINE

Moral Standards

There is a possibly apocryphal story that Sir Keith Joseph once asked officials at the Education Department why he should not introduce a national curriculum. They explained, at length, all the reasons, constitutional, traditional and practical, which made it impossible. He is reputed to have listened in silence, and finally observed: 'I do see. And of course you might always get a Secretary of State who was mad.'

Sir Keith, if he did say this, had put his finger on a key problem posed by the national curriculum and the directive power of the Minister. It confers enormous power to influence the ideas, values and judgements that are part of a school's life.

There is a possibility that, without realising it, Kenneth Baker is actually requiring teachers to teach their pupils to be like him. Kenneth Baker studied grammar. So shall everyone else. He and the Prime Minister learned their tables. It must be a good idea. The Minister is a Christian. There will be a Christian assembly in every school daily.

I remember attending a very stormy meeting in a primary school in East London which had been called by the head to discuss the conduct of daily assembly. Some parents had complained that the Lord's Prayer was not said each day during assembly. You might consider this dispute in a small primary school – which ended amicably enough – to be a little local difficulty. Not a bit of it. A contingent from Fleet Street, including reporters from the

Evening Standard, *Daily Mail* and *Daily Express*, attended. Several stories appeared in the national press before and after the meeting.

The meeting, of course, had a hidden agenda. A rumour had been spread among parents by an extreme right wing group that the school was going to become multiracial. In this case the desire for a daily recitation of the Lord's Prayer was in fact a coded demand for an all-white school. As it happened, there was no possibility of the school changing its predominantly white racial composition, which reflected that of its local area. Instead of the Lord's Prayer being recited every day, rather beautiful prayers and meditations written with younger audiences in mind were read out. The Archdeacon explained that the danger of using the Lord's Prayer too often was that the children would no longer hear the words they repeated so regularly. A member of the Conservative opposition and I explained that on this issue there was no political difference between us. We both supported the head and the Archdeacon.

The parents had initially been dissatisfied with the response to their complaint, perhaps because it did not relate to their unspoken anxiety. As so often happens, communication restored a sense of goodwill and mutual confidence, and the meeting broke up reasonably contentedly.

That particular school may not have been multiracial, but our society is. The languages spoken in London make it probably the most cosmopolitan city in the world. In many other parts of the country too the population is composed of British subjects of very different ethnic origins. We have become a multi-faith society. How are schools to respond to that? After all, what could be more fundamental than the faith by which a person lives?

The Education Reform Act lays a duty upon governors, heads and LEAs to ensure that an act of Christian worship takes place each day in State schools. That is a mistake. Of course it is sensible that the children and adults should gather together to collectively express their feelings on moral and social issues and to sing songs. I myself can clearly recall attending assembly at school and seeing Roman Catholic girls sitting outside the hall while it took place. I remember feeling in a childish way that there must be something a little strange about them. No one should be excluded in a multi-faith society. It is divisive to require that Christianity be given such a central position by legislation, particularly as many parents do not themselves regularly engage in collective worship.

Faced with this issue at ILEA, both in relation to assemblies and to religious education, we felt, as politicians, that the wisest course was to look to the churches themselves for guidance on this most sensitive matter. I reconvened the Standing Advisory Council on Religious Education (SACRE), and asked that body to draw up guidelines for the schools and an agreed religious education syllabus. Representatives of all the major faiths, including humanists, served on this body. The resulting document was unanimously agreed by SACRE and unanimously endorsed by representatives of all political parties on ILEA itself. It is of interest, I think, to quote the aims the church leaders felt appropriate for the teaching of religion in school: 'The aim is to help young people to achieve a knowledge and understanding of religious insight, beliefs and practices so that they are able to continue or come to their own beliefs and respect the right of other people to hold beliefs different from their own. While it is taken for granted that Christianity features prominently, the syllabus also provides for teaching about other important faiths which are held in contemporary British society. It is no part of the responsibility of the County School to provide any particular religious standpoint.'

I believe that we, as members of ILEA, were wise to stay out of the question of religious education, and that the church leaders who composed that inspiring document had a superior sense of what was right and appropriate to that contained in the Education Act.

A question connected with the faith we live by is that of how we see the world geographically and historically, and the place and contribution of our own society within it. This question is particularly sensitive in this country. I remember receiving an early geography lesson from my mother, who showed me an old map of the world which had various countries coloured pink to denote that they were British 'possessions'. My mother commented on the fading of imperial power. 'The lion is growing old,' she told me sadly.

Within the living memory of many of the population Britain's status has altered from that of imperial super-power to a European power of the second rank. This does not matter only to British leaders and statesmen. Working people fought in the colonial wars and in the two great territorial wars that have taken place in Europe this century. A widespread identification with the imperial vision has resulted, too often including a lack of respect for people who are not white and do not speak English as their first language.

What we think of one another in a multiracial society, what we think about other countries, what we think of our past and the possibilities of the present and the future are all interrelated questions with which the teachers have to deal.

In Michael Heseltine's book *Where There's a Will*, he recalls that when Harold Macmillan announced in Parliament in 1963 the Conservative Government's decision to apply to enter the Common Market, one of his own backbenchers shouted 'Traitor'. 'It showed he had done violence to some deep feelings and he faced a hard fight,' comments Heseltine.[1]

This 'little Englander' mentality persists. Mrs Thatcher has been described by the *Evening Standard* as 'the single greatest obstacle to Britain's participation in the European Economic Community . . . [She] appears to equate the EEC flattening of frontiers with a personal invasion of privacy.'

Meanwhile the gradual dismantling of barriers to the movement of trade and people continues. A number of absolutely practical questions are raised by this commercial process – and by the possibility of increased trade to the East. The political rhetoric masks this.

At its very simplest, as British firms expand across Western Europe, opportunities become available for British people to live and work in Germany, Italy, Spain or France either for British firms or for indigenous companies. In these circumstances the question of language teaching has to be taken seriously.

The contrast between our approach and that of other European countries could not be more marked. In 1978 I was involved in hosting an official dinner for civil servants and others attending a meeting of the Energy Council in Brussels. My co-host had had a good public school education, and I had attended an excellent girls' grammar school, but neither of us felt confident enough of our French – theoretically the international language of diplomacy – to converse in that language over dinner. So, via the Foreign Office intermediary who arranged the event, we made it clear as hosts that English would be spoken. Our German, Danish and Italian guests arrived first. What was striking to an English person was not simply the fluency and elegance of their English but that they spoke each other's languages too, so that they were able to slip in and out of different languages with equal facility. Gradually other guests arrived. The French were last. The elegant graduate of a Paris Haute Ecole entered approximately half an hour after everyone else. In faultless English he apologised for his inability to speak the language of his hosts and hoped that those present would not object to speaking French that evening. So saying, he launched into a critique in French of the events of the day: the other diners switched automatically to their fluent French. The British delegation were tongue-tied.

There is no excuse for this. Of course English is currently

the *lingua franca* of the trading world, but we should not rely on that. Why, if accomplished linguists can be turned out from Continental schools, can we not achieve the same results?

But how much commitment and energy will a 'little Englander' Government devote to promoting multi-lingualism, recognising foreign qualifications and financing regular exchanges with other countries?

Our place in Europe calls into question the basis of our study of subjects such as history. The traditional approach tends to be severely nationalistic. We pat ourselves on the back about Wellington at Waterloo, about Nelson at Trafalgar, about Montgomery at Alamein. Were there any great European men who were not British? Were there any great women of *any* nationality? Is nothing in the history of Europe over the last thousand years more important than glorifying our successes in territorial wars?

Of course few self-respecting history teachers would see European history in quite these terms. There must be a real fear that the central control of the national curriculum by a Government whose predisposition is traditional and nationalistic, and which is opposed to the kind of change which is actually taking place, will stand in the way of the developments I have described.

If our history makes it difficult for us to participate in Europe, our identity as a former colonial power makes it hard for us to perceive the history and geography of the world in a way which the inhabitants of other countries – and many of the people of this country – would find acceptable.

Many pupils from ethnic minority groups in this country also feel themselves to be a part of other communities elsewhere in the world. Children sitting in British classrooms may know from their own experience what everyday life is like in Hong Kong, or Jamaica, or India, or Africa, and their everyday experience may be more cosmopolitan than that of their teacher.

Sensitivities are bound to arise in the presentation of global relationships in the present day. Even more difficult will be a classroom historical perspective which narrates the development of the United Kingdom as an inspiring saga of individual initiative, exploration and conflict. The story of the European colonisation of the Americas and the colonial competition between the European powers in Africa may not seem so impressive to young people with families living in other parts of the world. We take the credit for abolishing the slave trade, yet we initiated and developed it. We may think that we graciously gave up our empire, yet other nations believe they fought heroically to expel us.

Questions of historical perspective also relate to the choice of writers to be studied in school. An old Schools Council document, 'Education of Children From Ethnic Minority Groups', puts it rather well:

Teachers will have to weigh very carefully arguments on both sides; to consider what will best help pupils to benefit and develop from their future experiences; under the traditional system they have probably not necessarily encountered all European musicians or authors, possibly coming to Palestrina and Monteverdi, to Beaumont and Fletcher and Lady Mary Wortley Montagu as adults, but have been able to place them in a historical perspective. Could they equally come to Arabian or Japanese composers, or to the works of Braithwaite or Ekwensi without some acquaintance at school with a wide variety of modes of artistic expression: if their historical experience has been limited to the British Isles and the Commonwealth, will they be able to react with under-standing to the changes that are taking place in the Middle East or South America?

Perhaps the kind of dilemma faced by teachers is best indicated by the legal requirement that in all matters that might be deemed 'political', teachers should represent both points of view. Very laudable, you might say, and in general I would agree. But should teachers present children with arguments in support of totalitarian regimes? Should they be legally obliged to put the arguments of those who support apartheid to a multiracial class? Under the current state of the law this is a real dilemma.

I have been engaged in a lengthy and unsatisfactory correspondence with the Inner London Education Authority over delays in printing a booklet entitled 'Learning About Apartheid' prepared by the British Defence and Aid Fund for Southern Africa which simply lists the source material available. Legal advice has had to be sought and a carefully worded introduction composed before ILEA could be associated with such a document. The obstacle was the apparent lack of political balance in such a publication.

The faith by which we live, our view of the world and our place in it and the assessment of our own past are complex matters, and teachers face sensitive decisions about how to treat them.

Perhaps the most sensitive issue of all is that of the roles people play, as men or women, black or white, in relation to each other and in terms of responsibility in the workplace.

Society exerts enormous pressure on people to be 'normal', to conform to well-established, stereotypical views of how categories of people should behave. The strongest pressure of all comes from the Government.

Parent governors will have to be brave in defence of the right to personal freedom and self expression of students in their schools.

There are difficult questions which parents on governing bodies need to face and resolve. On a simple level the head, when drawing up the timetable, will have to decide whether girls and boys will both study cookery and needlework and other practical subjects such as woodwork and metalwork. By that choice the school will make a major statement about the way it will educate men and women to behave. The roles played within the school by women and men teachers and by ethnic minority teachers will also say much about how the school sees a civilised society operating. The personal manners the teachers use to address their pupils are among the most important lessons in civilised conduct any school can offer. The recognition of discrimination and the ability to carry through sensible programmes to counter it are critical examples.

We are more aware today of the complexity of relationships in the adult and family world than ever before. Many children will live with divorced parents or parents who did not marry. Some parents abuse their children. Not all children will grow up to establish a conventional heterosexual relationship. A proportion will be homosexual. The availability of drugs, alcohol and the threat of diseases such as Aids place great burdens of responsibility on heads and teachers to warn and educate.

The presence of parents on the governing bodies of schools should itself be an assurance that a careful course acceptable to both parents and teachers will be shared on these sensitive matters. However, a recent Inspectorate Report warned that schools often did not prepare and plan the social and moral education of children in a sufficiently professional way. Although they allayed the fear that somehow individual teachers were advocating particular lifestyles or personal attitudes, their concern was rather that, compared with the preparation of academic syllabuses, the courses in personal education were underprepared.

There is a wider question. Schools exist in a society full of conflict, and are subject to the stress that accompanies change. Nowhere is this more true than in Britain, whose transition from the status of a world power to a European economy of the second rank has been extraordinarily swift.

The curricular philosophy that is being imposed on our schools with regard to the faiths that we live by, the analysis of the world we live in and the morality of our personal relations will not prepare children for the world they will actually inhabit. Professional even-handedness on these questions is preferable to requiring conformity by teachers to a particular set of individual views. This issue, with its important implications for intellectual and personal freedom, has yet to be resolved.

The national curriculum totally neglects personal abilities which are vital in the adult world. Its framework of thought is traditional, even reactionary, and could severely handicap children in their attempts to make sense of their personal lives. Most worryingly of all, it does not even attempt to prepare young people for participating in their own communities, for acting as citizens, for reaching out beyond their jobs and their homes. It is this narrowness which is the greatest flaw in what should have been an important reform. The definition of a curriculum as a mere list of academic studies is one-dimensional. It ignores areas such as equality of opportunity which thread across subject timetables and inform the life of a school. It ignores processes such as work experience, which provide an additional dimension to a child's education (see diagram, p. 156). Indeed, the national curriculum is not yet a curriculum at all. It is a subject timetable. This gives rise to the fear that the real purpose of the national curriculum is to provide a standardised set of ideas which will in turn form the basis for the standardised examinations which every pupil will sit.

TEN

Segregated Schools

The Government is putting a great deal of effort into tests and examinations. Kenneth Baker set up a special task group under Professor Black to advise him how to devise a national system of testing at the ages of 7, 11, 14 and 16. This task group reported in December 1987. Perhaps surprisingly, the Report, often called the TGAT (Task Group on Assessment and Testing), was acclaimed by the teaching profession.

The first question to ask about the Report is what the Government wanted testing to do. The next question is whether the system suggested by the Task Group will do what the Government wanted. The final question is whether there are other purposes to which the testing might be put, for example selection for secondary education places, whether this is the Government's intention or not.

It is difficult to ascertain exactly what Kenneth Baker had in mind when he set up the Task Group. The terms of reference were very wide, seeking advice 'on the practical consideration that should govern all assessment including testing of attainment at age (approximately) 7, 11, 14 and 16 within a national curriculum'. However, this was followed by a detailed letter in which Mr Baker told the Task Group exactly what he wanted them to provide him with. He certainly did not want general advice. He wanted a system of testing which provided results, or 'benchmarks', which could be used to tell how well a student had done; information which could be published so that parents could judge the education service; ways of aggregating results that would be useful to a wider public than the teacher, pupil or parent; and diagnostic tools that would show what remedial action was necessary to bring a pupil up to scratch. Furthermore, the tests were there to raise standards. This latter aim obviously occurred to Kenneth Baker as an afterthought, because it is included in neither the terms of reference or in his letter to the Task Group, but was a constant theme in his subsequent talks and speeches.

The Task Group suggested that in every subject there were five or six key components, and identified these in English, for example, as reading, writing, listening, comprehending and speaking. The next job is to identify the variety of knowledge, skills and understanding (and presumably anything else that can be thought of such as competencies, attitudes and abilities) that make up each component of each subject and list them hierarchically. These hierarchical lists are then to be divided into ten levels. For each component there has to be teacher assessment which can be of whatever type is felt appropriate so long as it is properly moderated by a complicated system of regional groups meeting together under a teacher acting as regional Chair. Alongside this complex system of regional groups, busily meeting together to moderate for all their worth, there is to be a national standardised test for each component. When the teacher assessment and the national test do not agree, there should be extra tests available to decide the matter. The results of the duly moderated teacher assessment and the standardised national test are to be added together to give each student a mark which will show that student's level.

The following table, which is taken from the TGAT Report, shows how students will be judged in each component. The average level for students aged 7 will be somewhere between 1 and 3, while for a student aged 11 it will be between 3 and 6. At the age of 14 students will be somewhere between 4 and 8. Finally, at the age of 16, a student will be between 4 and 10. Notice that GCSE grades A to F fall between levels 7 and 10.

Table 6: Sequence of Pupil Achievement of Levels Between Ages 7 and 16

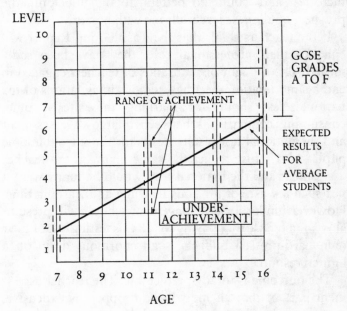

Source: Task Group Report on Assessment and Testing, January 1988

This system looks like an imaginative attempt to do what the Secretary of State asked. It is rather like one of those puzzles where you are given a number of squares and asked to construct a triangle. The result is the fruit of a great deal of ingenuity, but what on earth can be done with it?

Even assuming that the components in each subject can be defined, and a list of skills and understandings devised for each component and put into a hierarchy, how do you even begin to bring all these together to decide which level a child is on at the age of 7? Perhaps the 7-year-old will be put at a different level for each of the ten subjects in the national curriculum. Or is it a different level for each component in each of the ten subjects of the national curriculum, a total of fifty or sixty levels? While I have always found the traditional report, with its lists of 'satis-factories' and 'could do betters' totally unhelpful, the prospect of all these levels fills me with horror.

If the teachers think that the Task Group Report will enhance their professional role, they have been sadly misled. The thought of thousands of teachers engaged in endless moderation meetings, tedious invigilations of the national test, hours of marking these tests, time-consuming comparisons between their own assessment and the national test results, resits for those troublesome pupils who refuse to get the same mark on the teacher assessment and the national test, would be funny were it not such a waste of precious teaching and learning time. However, under local management schools will presum-ably soon realise that paying for all this testing out of their own hard-pressed budgets is an enormous drain on a limited resource.

The outcome is totally predictable. The teacher assess-ment part of the scheme will be dropped as expensive, complicated and unworkable and the country will be left with standardised tests as the credible alternative. At first sight this may not appear such a bad thing. However, the implications should be explored.

When the national curriculum is specified in terms of subjects it would appear that these benchmarks and the tests that underlie them are actually a way of reinforcing the national curriculum. It is an extraordinary assumption that subjects can be broken down in the way the Task Group has suggested. It is even more difficult to order the skills and knowledge that make up the components in hierarchical piles suggesting what a student ought to be able to do in each subject at each age. The reality is that the range of what can be done at each age is enormous;

learning is not necessarily age-related, nor are subjects necessarily hierarchical. Many people have already tried to point this out to the Secretary of State for Education and Science.

His reaction has been to reject the advice. Clearly the Government is looking for a detailed subject syllabus to be imposed on all State schools, though not on public schools, through a national testing system. It has already been argued that a subject-based national curriculum is not necessarily appropriate. It therefore seems equally objectionable to impose a syllabus to go with that national curriculum through testing. This is what happened under the 'payment by results' system in the nineteenth century, which, when set alongside the Government's ideological commitment to the market solution, suggests a future scenario. Schools will win their students on the basis of the results that they can demonstrate, and will thus gain or lose money through the results of national standardised tests. If local government becomes a thing of the past, the Government will have a ready-made funding criterion.

If schools are to be compared by examination and test results it is absolutely vital that steps are taken to measure progress rather than relative achievement. This is important, because a school which caters for students with every disadvantage might actually do more for its students than a school in a leafy suburb where the students have every advantage. A comparison of raw scores might suggest that the suburban school was better; this would be a measure of student achievement. However, if the advantages and disadvantages of the students were taken into account, the suburban school might be shown to be doing worse; this would be a measure of progress or value added by the school.

If there is one thing that has been clearly demonstrated over the last thirty years, it is that test results reflect the degree of advantage or disadvantage in the background and upbringing of individual children. The Statistics

Branch of the Department of Education and Science came
to the conclusion that socio-economic background was the
biggest determinant of examination success. Of course
there will always be individuals who succeed despite their
disadvantages. What we cannot do is to justify a system
which precipitates the vast majority of children into a
second-class educational experience on the basis of their
socio-economic background just because a few succeed in
breaking through these barriers. Children from disadvantaged socio-economic backgrounds almost invariably start
their school careers at a lower level of achievement than
their more advantaged peers. They rarely if ever succeed in
catching up, but they may make as much progress as those
with every advantage.

Clearly, then, progress rather than relative achievement
should be measured if a true comparison is to be made.
This would entail a massive data collection exercise cou-
pled with a great deal of statistical research analogous to
the work that has taken place in ILEA, which has issued
school examination results based on progress not achievement. So far the Government has taken no steps to collect
the appropriate data, so it looks as if it wants schools to be
compared on bogus results which provide no real comparison.

If tests are to be used to compare schools, the key
question is whether these tests are actually intended to
assess the work of the adults in the school, or to help the
adults to monitor the work of the children. These are
linked but separate processes.

There are very few educationalists who believe that one
test can serve both purposes. Either there must be two
different kinds of test or one purpose will be inadequately
fulfilled. The Task Group on Assessment and Testing has
either failed to recognise this, or is deliberately deceiving
us.

It is difficult to know what the Government means by
the claim that tests raise standards. They may well raise the

standards of test-taking, as teachers carefully train their students to do well in the tests, but this does not mean that educational standards are raised. Tests can only encompass a limited range of the kind of educational objectives that have been discussed in previous chapters. Furthermore, to be practicable and feasible, a national test will have to be written. Even some of those charged with devising national tests have said that there are other kinds of tests, for example oral or practical, which are more appropriate. This is particularly true where 7-year-olds are concerned, since their reading ability is very limited.

Where schools are judged by their results, where their clientele or their budgets are dependent on the score attained in a nationalised test, there is a definite advantage for a school in obtaining the best students it can – or at least the students who are best at sitting standardised national tests. There is every danger that the test results will thus serve another purpose. They will enable the best schools to select the best students. The prospect of the national testing system being the new 7+, 11+, 14+ and 16+ is with us. As things stand it would be difficult for schools to throw out students who do not make the grade to be replaced by students who have achieved higher scores in the national test, but with the decline of local education authority influence and the development of City Technology Colleges, Grant Maintained Schools or more fee paying schools, this may well happen.

In conclusion, it should be said that public accountability requires that schools should be assessed, and that assessment should be quantified. This is part of an LEA's system to help it identify where there may be cause for concern. Such assessment should be of progress. It should not define the curriculum. The work of children should be monitored, and this presents an entirely different problem. It would be far more constructive to concentrate more effort on graded assessment, rather in the mode of some music

certificates, where students can take the test when they are
ready. It would also be helpful to speed work on devising
curriculum modules so that students could work on short
parts of courses which build up into a complete course.
This would help to escape the straitjacket of thought
which assumes that knowledge is hierarchical.

More important for the individual student than all of
this is to move towards an assessment system based on a
record of achievement. Again considerable progress has
been made in ILEA, and it was decided that by 1990 every
fifth-year student in every ILEA secondary school will leave
or move into post-compulsory education with a London
Record of Achievement. This is a portfolio which contains
a student statement, in which the students reflect on their
achievements and interests; a school statement which gives
a picture of the positive achievements of the student;
samples of the student's work; and all certificates, examination results and other formal qualifications and
achievements. The London Record of Achievement is the
actual folder that the students can take with them when
seeking further education or employment. Backing up the
folder is the profiling system, which generates counselling
and appraisal between teacher and student, the setting of
goals, the analysis of weaknesses, formal and informal
discussion with parents and guardians, the celebration of
success and a great deal of thought and negotiation on the
curriculum. The idea of a profile and the system of profiling embodied in the London Record of Achievement is a
far more constructive way to raise standards and improve
accountability than a hugely complex and expensive system of national testing which is of doubtful validity, may
actually be educationally harmful, and which looks suspiciously like the reintroduction of selection and payment
by results.

How far does the whole strategic plan provide for the
reform of the public education service? Will the franchise
system of management, the national curriculum and the

testing programme together improve our schools? Will it resolve the crisis in public management?

As a strategy for raising standards it will not work. It is in conflict with the financial strategy, which is designed to produce a stratified system. Within its own terms it is inadequate; a franchise system tends towards uniformity, not quality. It is based on a faulty educational analysis which fails to recognise that a much more sophisticated system of quality monitoring is required. Finally, it lacks a strategic context derived from the immediate needs of society.

The standardised mass testing of children at the ages of 7, 11, 14 and 16 years would be a catastrophe. Presumably intended to serve the purposes of selection, it is in fact a system of planned economic inequality based on a reactionary analysis of the distribution of intelligence amongst children. It is simply a mechanism for allocating differentially funded schooling between different social groups. It is ethically and educationally indefensible, and has no relevance to measuring and improving the general standard of education.

The disadvantages and pitfalls in the Government's plans prompt the obvious reflection that there must be a simpler, better way to organise our schools. What is that alternative?

ELEVEN

There is an Alternative

For nearly ten years, a central illusion of British public life has been that there is no alternative to the policies of the Government, and that, however pointlessly destructive these policies may appear, they are mystically in tune with a natural process of economic death and rebirth. They arise, it is claimed, out of the extension of freedom and the exercise of choice within the framework of the Government's will. They are destined to be successful.

In fact, there is an alternative to the Government's education policy, which derives from a different philosophical, economic and educational perspective. Education is so important that such an alternative deserves to be rationally assessed.

What then is this alternative? In part it is philosophical. Government Ministers have stressed their libertarian vision of freedom, supported by the theories of Hayek, as if one thinker could provide sufficient resource for such a vision. In fact, a small number of great geniuses have told us most of what we know about human life and the universe. Einstein, Darwin, Marx, Freud, perhaps Adam Smith, perhaps Keynes, have bequeathed us a massive intellectual legacy. All of them raised more questions than they answered. None offered simple truths, nor even simple plans for human institutions. We live in a world illuminated by their insights, but also by our own experience. Hayek, a single thinker working within the tradition of Adam Smith, warned that institutions of public planning could frustrate the objectives they were set up to achieve, and in the process frustrate the freedom of individuals. His case is well made, but it is possible to draw different conclusions from it.

Children are not born equal. Not only do their abilities vary, but the distribution of life chances among our child population varies massively. Earlier, I described the extent and effects of that uneven distribution. The libertarian vision of freedom, translated into a market system of schools, will simply reinforce that maldistribution, in the way I described in Chapter 4. This alternative starting point gives rise to a different definition of freedom, linked to the goal of equality of opportunity. It is framed to meet and to absorb Hayek's case. Freedom, for the children of an unequal society, *must* be planned.

The alternative philosophical perspective is obvious, and in my opinion ethically superior. It deserves restating.

The freedom of every child to learn, develop, grow and make choices about their life is inseparable from access to schooling. That schooling must be paid for out of the public purse, otherwise the extent of the child's access will be conditioned by parental income.

The freedom of every child to develop their ability to the full depends on the existence of a planned comprehensive system, otherwise the child's development will be primarily determined by social background, reinforced by the selective pattern of schooling.

The freedom of every child to excel depends on their attending a school as good as the best schools that exist, otherwise the school itself will set limits on the achievement of the pupils within it.

Among the controlling principles of a school system designed to offer equality of opportunity to *every* child is that it should be free at the point of use. Can we afford such a system? Here I diverge from the view of Ministers, who claim that they are pursuing a radically different economic strategy from that of previous administrations. This strategy, they argue, necessitates annual reductions in spending on public services such as education. This is not in fact true. Certainly the Government was initially elected on a platform of Friedmanite economic management. Of that programme only the rhetoric remains. The abandoning of the monetarist plan is discussed in Chapter 3. Meanwhile the British economy continues to grow much as it did before. We continue to grow richer as a society every year, and we continue to be vulnerable to crises within the financial markets as we were in 1976.

In these circumstances it is the increase in the overall level of spending, private and public, that has to be carefully managed if inflation, a trade deficit and a currency crisis are to be avoided. Within the management of growth there is no economic reason for cutting public spending while increasing the level of private expenditure. Indeed, investment in education is itself a key economic goal. Public and private spending can and should be allowed to increase in parallel.

In practice that means that the Government can and should gradually increase the percentage contribution from national taxation to the local school systems so that the level of the poll tax can in turn be reduced. Schooling can be free. An adequate level of books and equipment can be provided. Teachers can share in the increase in personal wealth.

Controls on borrowing and capital spending by local education authorities can be relaxed, and our decaying school buildings repaired, repainted and modernised. This is *not* a perspective of unplanned growth in the post-war manner, but of gradual, planned improvements. It is the alternative to the present demoralising and unnecessary contraction. The system of a well-funded education service free at the point of use offering economic equality of opportunity envisaged by Rab Butler is perfectly possible within current economic constraints.

What strategy, and what structure of schooling, will result from this perspective? A second basic principle is the need for a planned comprehensive system. Ministers have argued that a planned, egalitarian system must almost by virtue of being planned inevitably fail. Yet there is a substantial body of hard empirical evidence, largely ignored by the critics of the public education service, which provides a very clear guide to a successful egalitarian schooling system. Contrary to prevailing mythology it does not require a choice between the efficient use of resources, high levels of attainment by pupils and careful monitoring of quality.

For example, evidence shows that the single most effective way of improving the standards of attainment of all pupils, and in particular of helping children from disadvantaged homes, would be to provide nursery school places for all. An important omission from Kenneth Baker's plan is any provision for the education of under-fives. Mrs Thatcher, when Education Minister, had some sympathy for the need to expand this sector. She published a White Paper, 'Education: A Framework for Expansion', which required that local authorities provide nursery places for 90 per cent of 4-year-olds and 50 per cent of 3-year-olds.[1] The plan was never implemented. Today, as Prime Minister, she would probably say that the education of children up to the age of 5 is the responsibility of their families. Such a statement chimes with her well-known views on self-reliance and self-respect and the superiority of people's own attempts to help themselves to relying on that which the State can provide.

There has, historically, been another reason for the Government's silence – unwillingness to pay. One evening in June 1984 I shared a platform with Sir Keith Joseph, then Education Minister, at Central Hall, Westminster. The occasion was a parents' rally to celebrate the 40th anniversary of the 1944 Education Act. I publicly asked Sir Keith why, if he was so concerned about standards, he was not developing a nursery sector. One of Sir Keith's impressive qualities as a politician is his frankness. In answering my question he did not trouble to dissimulate either by suggesting that nursery education was unnecessary or that most children already received it. 'The British economy is not successful enough to pay for nursery schools,' he replied tersely.

No reputable educationalist would dispute that by the age of 5 – the official starting age of formal education – children from poorer homes will enter school at a marked disadvantage to children of professional parents, and that the gap will progressively widen during the school life of both groups of children.

Pre-school education makes a measurable difference to that early handicap. In 1970, for example, two British researchers, Albert Osborn and Janet Milbank, began a study of every child born in England and Wales in a single week in April of that year.[2] The researchers asked a single question: 'Could pre-school education have a beneficial effect on the intellectual development, educational achievement and behaviour of the children concerned?' The answer was a resounding 'yes'. Children who had attended a local authority nursery school – not nursery class! – achieved measurably higher scores in reading and mathematics in primary school than those who had not. If we accept these findings it seems to me inescapable that the first step in raising standards would involve providing pre-school education for all.

Oddly enough, quite conservative American politicians seem clearer about this issue than our own Government. John Ashcroft, Governor of the State of Missouri, has said: 'Human resources in the State of Missouri happen to be developable and expandable. If I were to tell you that I could develop and expand the amount of oil beneath the surface of my State you would laugh at me. But the resource is more important than oil.' Missouri, a state with a poor standard of education, took advice from leading educationalists who emphasised to the Governor the view that the early environment of a child has a huge effect on what that child can later learn and achieve. In 1981 the Parents as Teachers project was piloted in four of the education districts of the state. It is described in an entertaining book by Jane Walmsley and Jonathan Margolis, *Hothouse People*.[3] Prevention rather than cure was the aim of this carefully and independently monitored experiment. It was designed to deal with the fact that by the age of 3 many children have already fallen so severely behind in their personal development that their progress in later life is jeopardised.

The four districts conducted a three-year programme in which 'trainers' worked with parents, teaching them how to teach their babies. The children whose parents participated were reported, by 3 years of age, to show substantial mental and linguistic progress by comparison with children who did not participate. The involvement of parents was, the scheme designers believe, the crucial factor in the scheme's success.

It is particularly interesting to compare that evidence with the findings of our own British research project. In both cases all the children benefited, but the most disadvantaged benefited most of all.

When Sir Keith Joseph was a Minister at the Department of Health and Social Security in 1970–74 (before he became a monetarist!) he used to talk about the 'cycle of deprivation'. This is the process whereby children of poor, uneducated parents who live in overcrowded conditions and work at lowly paid occupations have children who fail in school and themselves go on to live in poor housing and do low-income jobs. This is the process tracked in detail in the National Children's Bureau's study 'From Birth to Seven'. Sir Keith used to wonder how we could break that cycle. It seems that under-5 provision could actually make a contribution towards avoiding the sad process whereby the working-class child enters school as full of hope as his or her middle-class counterpart but emerges having 'failed', and could also benefit all other children.

Attendance at a good primary school can also increase the attainment of all children, and in particular that of disadvantaged pupils according to the Junior School Project led by Dr Peter Mortimer and published in 1986/87.[4] What is a good primary school? Quite simply, it is a well-managed school. Dr Mortimer identifies twelve factors. The first of these is the 'purposeful leadership' of the head, defined as 'understanding the needs of the school, and [being] actively involved in the school's work without exerting total control over the rest of the staff . . . influencing the teaching style of teachers but only selectively . . . instituting a systematic policy of record keeping'.

The effectiveness of the school also rested in part on the capacity of the deputy head. 'Where the deputy was frequently ill or absent for a prolonged period' there was evidence that the pupils' progress suffered, and a change of deputy of itself had a negative effect. The way staff worked together in the school also contributed to the quality of the education it provided: in schools where the teachers were involved in decisions about curriculum planning and spending, the policies were more successful.

A calm and structured environment was important. Teachers who 'organised a framework within which pupils could work' were much more successful than those who offered the children unlimited responsibility for choosing their own work. Intellectually challenging teaching was also effective as opposed to direction without discussion, or interrogation about progress. A high level of pupil industry, a low noise level and a minimum of pupil movement around the classroom were important elements in what made a school work. Careful records of pupils' work progress, parental involvement in the school, the degree to which it had a positive ethos, 'the organisation of lunchtime and after school clubs for pupils; teachers eating lunch at the same tables as children: organisation of trips or visits and the use of the local environment as a learning resource' all helped create an effective school.

What the Junior School Project shows is that schools do make a difference, and that a good school makes a difference to all the groups within it.

Very similar findings come from a recently published ten-year study of 40,000 pupils in Scotland in the 1970s and 1980s which shows that comprehensive reorganisation has helped to improve standards of examination attainment. The study, conducted by the Centre for Educational Sociology (CES) at Edinburgh University, is the largest and most up-to-date investigation of comprehensive schooling in Britain, following the fortunes of three quarters of Scotland's secondary schools over an eight-year period. Its other main finding is that schooling has in fact started to produce a fairer balance of opportunity. Since the mid-1970s the social-class gap in attainment has narrowed, and the attainment of middle-class pupils has improved. The trends are evident for boys and girls alike, but the attainment of girls has improved even more than that of boys.

Part of the reason for the delay in obtaining clear evidence of the effect of comprehensive reorganisation is the time that was taken for the system to become fully operational. Only in the mid-1970s did the Scottish public system become fully comprehensive. Between 1945 and 1975 educational attainment in Scotland followed a pattern which coincided with social class. In other words, the education system was not able to overcome the effects of social disadvantage. Ten years after the system went comprehensive, a break in that pattern became evident: comprehensive education in Scotland, by improving the attainment of the working-class child, while at the same time improving the attainment of the middle-class child, had demonstrated that it was possible to have both quality and equality, to safeguard the interests of the able and to lay the foundations of a fairer society.

The study found that comprehensive reorganisation gave Scottish schools a more representative mixture of children from all social classes than did a tripartite system. It also found that the achievements of the pupils improved the longer the school had been an all-through comprehensive rather than part of a system which included selective schools. Of course the Scottish comprehensive system did not eliminate the pattern of attainment related to social class, but it did break the apparently rigid relationship between social class and attainment, and made the system fairer.

These major longitudinal studies, the Junior School Project and the Edinburgh University study of Scottish comprehensives have both reached the same conclusions. The educational environment can alter, and has altered, the patterns of achievement of groups: greater equality is possible. Furthermore, greater equality can be achieved at the same time as an improvement in quality.

Freedom, equality, economic efficiency and an increase in standards of attainment *can* be achieved by a comprehensive schooling system within a framework of local authority planning.

Within such a sensible national system of schooling a national curriculum would take its proper place. Obviously the inflexibility of the current curriculum needs to be modified. The curriculum proposed by Kenneth Baker is one-dimensional. It needs to be developed to allow far greater flexibility of subject choices, to include the various threads that weave through the whole subject timetable, to incorporate the processes that make up a child's whole educational experience (see diagram, p. 156). A local authority role is needed to develop local curriculum initiatives – like the compacts between local schools and employers. Such initiatives could range from establishing local orchestras and sports teams to organising regular European exchanges. The key point is that a school's curriculum is strengthened and expanded by organised contact with the outside world as well as by what takes place within the school itself.

A free, planned comprehensive system can be afforded, and is desirable. But can it be managed? And can quality be ensured? These are the questions raised by a Hayekian analysis and by the Black Paper writers. They must be answered.

The development of a professional management within schools is desperately needed to deal with the most important flaw in the present system, namely the variation in the performance of schools despite similar intakes of pupils, numbers of staff and finance. Ministers seem to believe that by establishing a system of self-governing State schools to be managed from Whitehall, with the aid of mass testing, they have established such a system. They are wrong. Indeed, in the short term the shift to self-government by schools will intensify the management crisis that already exists.

Perhaps the first step in the creation of a management structure would be the establishment of a series of staff colleges to train all heads and senior teachers in the skills of professional management. We know that in many ways what is defined as a 'good' school is in reality a well-managed school. We also know that in a school which is not well managed the attainment of children suffers markedly. The world of public education is in this sense underdeveloped. Professional bodies like the Society of Education Officers would themselves admit their need for increased expertise in this area. If a head, deputy head and senior staff do happen to make up a good management team, it is by good fortune rather than good planning. This was the position when schools confined themselves to managing the educational programme. But management training will have to go far beyond that. By 1992 most local authority schools will be responsible for their own budgets. This will involve huge new managerial responsibilities. At present a typical secondary school may cost £3 million to £5 million a year to run, including the cost of staffing, heating, painting, cleaning and repairs as well as materials and books. The training programme will need to be extensive if it is to provide a major way of improving the quality of organisation of every school. Schools will need to undertake a comprehensive planning and budgeting process, which must provide opportunities to review education policies and must be carried out within a disciplined financial framework. Perhaps schools will set up budgetary committees. Appropriate skills will be required of the financial officer to ensure that decisions are properly costed and can be afforded. It will be vital to ensure that variations from the approved budget are detected early and that corrective action is taken. New school-based financial systems will be needed. Given that budgets will be directly related to pupil numbers, schools will see themselves as being in competition with other schools. A need to undertake cost comparison with other schools is likely to emerge.

Another example of new demand is in the area of probity. Proper management of increased financial resources, tenders and contracting and financial resources will all make demands on schools.

Schools may not require the services of a qualified accountant, but they will need staff trained in financial disciplines and procedures. Over and above the need to train heads and senior staff is the need to provide for financial management. There is at present no system of training for staff which relates to the new situation. A large number of people will be involved, and consideration should be given to the development of a training and accreditation programme specifically designed to meet their needs. Governors too will need training. Either local authorities will have to be responsible for this huge project, or a national agency will have to be created.

Educationalists have traditionally been sceptical about the role of management, preferring to emphasise the primacy of the classroom teacher. The whole purpose of developing professional management methods within schools is to ensure that the interaction between pupils and teachers – between the service and its clients – is carried out as well as possible.

Provided the shift to school self-government is accompanied by large-scale in-service management training, it is a welcome reform. But what about the management of the system? The removal of all major planning powers except responsibility for the capital budget from the local authorities is an error that needs to be rectified. No matter how professionally managed each school becomes, systematic monitoring of quality still needs to take place. Thousands of schools cannot be centrally monitored with the aid of a testing system run by the National Foundation for Educational Research.

Local education authorities have been freed to concentrate on a vital task that hitherto they have neglected – monitoring the quality of education being provided in each school in their area, and identifying schools whose pupils are not receiving a sufficiently high level of education offer. This monitoring role goes hand in hand with the responsibility of setting targets for low-achieving schools, and providing support to bring them to an acceptable standard. This is one of the basic functions of local education authorities. They should be given statutory powers to enable them to carry it out, and a statutory responsibility for maintaining quality in each school.

The critical question, of course, is how to assess the work of schools. Any method of evaluating schools on a comparative basis must be relatively simple, it must be fair, and it must convince the professionals as well as the parents of its validity. The complicated monitoring schemes, involving an enormous amount of teachers' time, a vital resource, as described in the Black Report, seem to me impractical. And standard tests are technically defective. They conceal real failure and real success by not comparing like with like. For example, the relative under-performance of a school with children from professional backgrounds is concealed by comparing that school with one in a very poor area. Conversely, the success of a school in a poor area may be concealed within the statistics.

The best method of assessment is one which would simultaneously provide a tool with which staff could appraise their own work and enable the local authorities to do the same. There are two complementary parts to such a system of assessment. The formal inspection of a school either by HMI or by a local inspectorate of equal standing and competence, reporting its findings to the staff, the governing body and the local authority is the vital first part. Every school should undergo such an inspection at least once every five years. A more quantified assessment can be provided by the assignment to the school of a target based on an educational assessment of each pupil upon entry and a comparison of results – for example in public examinations. Some might fear that such a process would diminish the ambitions of a school for its pupils. That depends on the targets. In principle, the reverse is the case, and the procedure would show up very clearly those schools which were overcoming environmental patterns of attainment and those which were not. By testing the school itself, it would avoid stigmatising the children.

If local authorities are to develop a clear responsibility for the impartial assessment of the quality of education by means of professional inspection and performance indicators, there seems every reason to include fee paying schools within the area in such a monitoring system. So long as public money, in the form of tax concessions and Assisted Places Schemes, goes into the private sector, the responsibility for auditing the quality it buys should be carried out by public institutions. Taxpayers have as much right to know the value for their money provided by the private as the public sector. Arguably, even in the desirable event of all public money being withdrawn from the private sector, the fee paying schools should still be required to submit to independent educational assessment, simply to ensure that parents are not being defrauded.

Essentially, public management must borrow the best practices of the private sector. A quantified assessment of the progress of each school measured against sensibly determined targets should form the basis of a yearly report publicly presented by local inspectors at the annual meeting of the local authority. These reports should be at least as important as the annual debate on the education budget, and should be accompanied by a parallel document from the education administration setting out its strategies for eliminating weaknesses and building on strengths within its service in the coming year. A report prepared by HMI should be presented by the Secretary of State for Education to Parliament. Such a process could lead to the proper management and monitoring of State schools, and to bringing the private sector under necessary scrutiny.

How should the work of children be assessed? Here I must confess to being a heretic about the examination of 16-year-olds by a system which a fixed percentage is not allowed to participate in, and which a fixed percentage is destined to fail. A system of public assessment modelled on that by which performance on a musical instrument is tested has always struck me as preferable. Assessment begins with simple tests, moving on to increasingly higher levels. The child progresses at his or her own pace, taking successive examinations when he or she is ready for them. At no single moment is a child classified definitively as a success or a failure.

A developed national curriculum, professionally managed schools whose work was assessed publicly each year, and a rational public examination system would go a long way towards creating a service in which each child has as good an education as the best available.

There are two provisos. The strategic jumble of educational arrangements beyond the age of 16 needs to be sorted out. The current split at national level in the organisation, administration and funding of education and training is not defensible. The sooner a unified national system is created, the easier it will be to start to create equality of opportunity at local level and to remove the frustration and waste caused by differentiation into exclusive educational or training channels at 16. The current split between the DES, the former Manpower Services Commission, renamed the Training Agency, and the Department of Employment must be healed by creating a Department of Education and Training.

We also need a national tertiary curriculum, which is an altogether more complex matter than the national secondary curriculum. The relationships with industry need to be developed so that industry can understand and where necessary influence that curriculum. More importantly, industry must develop a commitment to a comprehensive tertiary system which welcomes and responds to its concerns. Once again, local education authorities will have to be involved. The seeds are already being sown. Work has begun on a post-16 Development Plan. There is no reason why this cannot be expanded to form the tertiary curriculum plan. Secondly, the basis for a constructive industry–education relationship is there already. In ILEA and other parts of the country, formal and informal links between industry and further education colleges are very strong. In ILEA, for example, a business representative sits on the Post Schools Education Subcommittee, and the London Compact is beginning to explore the implications for post-compulsory education and training. The alternative to a comprehensive tertiary system is a rigidly structured system with no progression between phases, relying on market forces to determine industrial training needs.

And what of *style*, the way we do things, the intangible quality of thoughts, relationships and actions within a planned education system? It is here that I differ most profoundly from the Government. A recent report by HMI was prefaced by the remarkable statement: 'We are school inspectors, not investigators or detectives.'

The 1944 Education Act envisaged a partnership based on mutual respect between all those responsible for delivering the education service. The development of modern management skills within the service is not incompatible with this aim. Sporadic authoritarian gestures from Government or from local authorities are. For that reason I believe we should look not to the 1988 Act but to its great predecessor for our broad vision of the service. We should continue to follow the egalitarian path, but with a much clearer view of our destination.

The most enlightened of philosophies and the best of systems depend ultimately on the people who operate them. Teachers, as well as being one of the most important groups in the country, are probably one of the most alienated. Left for decades to sort out for themselves what went on in schools, they were then blamed by Government and local managements for failing to meet goals which had never been set. Fundamental to the reform of public education is the recognition that teaching is a profession which merits high status and high pay. Like, for example, the medical profession, it should be subject to a demanding qualification process. It should have an attractive career structure. I believe we should demand a great deal from our teachers, and offer them a great deal in return.

Conclusion

This book is about a strategy for schools which differs from that of the Government. The world of education of course exists far beyond the classroom. I have restricted myself to the statutory sector in order to follow the thread of argument through the maze of institutions, committees, Acts and Reports to its source. But the Government's strategy is of course being applied across the whole education service, and its objectives are the same.

Is it realistic to advocate that the Government strategy be opposed? I remember speaking in the Budget Debate one year at ILEA. Opposition Councillors had argued that if only ILEA would begin a programme of spending cuts, the Government would be appeased and would go away, and that, in any case, the Authority would be forced to reduce its spending one day. Surely it would be wise to start at once.

My fellow Councillors' speeches reminded me vividly of the legend of the Minotaur, which lived in the labyrinth on Crete and demanded every year the sacrifice of young maidens and men in return for leaving the rest of the population alone. There must have been sagacious Cretans who argued that things were not really so bad, as only a certain percentage of maidens and men were affected. In fairness to those who were to be spared, the choice of victims should be made early.

The Government's strategy for schools will certainly sacrifice the educational chances of at least a proportion of each generation of children. I feel that the sacrifice of even one child's education on the altar of competition is too high a price to pay.

I believe that, like Theseus and Ariadne, we should enter the labyrinth, confront the Minotaur and assert that there is such a thing as society, and that it has a duty to its children.

What then should Government do, in a world of self-governing schools within self-governing communities?

It should do what it ought to have done in the past – set goals, revise them, and regularly determine the broad strategy and structure of public education. Thereafter its primary responsibility is to guard the guardians.

It is *not* the Government's job to run the education service, as it is now trying to do. If it does, who is to assess what is being done? Kenneth Baker's repeal of his responsibility to present an annual report seems to indicate that there will be no serious external audit of the national management of resources, no detached and rigorous assessment of educational success or failure, and no public strategic debate, even within our determinedly amateur and enfeebled Parliamentary system.

Ultimately it is the willingness of Parliament, and particularly the House of Commons, to accept this mode of Government which too often reduces public discussion of major educational questions to competitive slogans prepared by public relations agencies.

The egalitarian political consensus that safeguarded public education needs to be recreated around a practical philosophical, economic and educational plan. In this book I have tried to contribute to that process. Virtually everything I have proposed within the alternative strategy has already been done, has already succeeded: it is from the best practice of the practitioners that we should derive our plans.

The leadership needed to rebuild that consensus will, I believe, need to come out of the education service too. We live in a democracy in which any Government is only as powerful as its citizens allow it to be. Even now, if those involved in governing bodies, in educational pressure groups, in staffrooms and parent-teacher associations came together to agree on the immediate needs of the education service and resolved to seek public support, they would be surprised at the extent to which they could affect Government policy.

Partly this depends on whether newly-powerful parents recognise the importance of their responsibilities. All children matter as much as their own. All schools count as much as the one for which they are responsible. It will not be easy for parents to overcome the 'divide and rule' school system which has been imposed on them. They will need to look to local authorities, national bodies and even political parties for guidance. Will they get it? The fracturing since 1976 of the consensus which bound together the egalitarian generation of political leaders and thinkers came about because the need for key reforms was not recognised. Every generation of parents in the post-war period has desired high-quality education for their children. That desire unified parents from all sectors of society. Yet since the 1970s their needs have not been taken into account by the professionals.

From personal experience I must say that it will take no less than an intellectual revolution within the political and professional institutions which make up the education world to bring about a coherent response to this heartfelt demand. Everything depends on whether the genuine devotion to public education which exists in that world can overcome the self-absorbed traditions which developed as the mirror-image of Government's amateurism and indifference. I hope that the education world will reunite around a credible plan for the high-quality, planned public service the country needs. The practitioners too carry a heavy responsibility. The whole public education service is held in trust by its custodians, not just for today but also for tomorrow, for the children of the future.

Appendix

Table 7: Summary of the effects of taxes and benefits, 1985

	Quintile groups of households ranked by original income					Average over all households
	Bottom	2nd	3rd	4th	Top	
Average per household (£ per year)						
Original income	120	2 720	7 780	12 390	22 330	9 070
plus cash benefits	3 260	2 570	1 200	790	670	1 700
Gross income	3 380	5 300	8 980	13 170	23 000	10 770
less income tax[1] and employees' NIC	-10[2]	360	1 460	2 560	5 300	1 930
Disposable income	3 390	4 940	7 530	10 610	17 700	8 830
less indirect taxes	790	1 420	2 050	2 640	3 840	2 150
Income after cash benefits and all taxes	2 590	3 520	5 480	7 970	13 860	6 680
plus benefits in kind	1 370	1 400	1 440	1 490	1 590	1 460
Final income	3 960	4 920	6 920	9 460	15 450	8 140
Percent that are public sector tenants	62	34	26	15	7	29
Average per household (number)						
Children (i.e. aged under 16)	0.4	0.4	0.8	0.8	0.6	0.6
Adults	1.4	1.7	2.0	2.2	2.7	2.0
People in full-time education	0.3	0.3	0.6	0.7	0.7	0.5
Economically active people	0.1	0.6	1.3	1.8	2.2	1.2
Retired people	0.8	0.8	0.2	0.1	0.1	0.4

[1] After tax relief at source on mortgage interest and life assurance premiums.
[2] Negative average tax payment results largely from imputed tax relief on life assurance premiums paid by those with nil or negligible tax liabilities.

Source: Institute for Fiscal Studies/Central Statistical Office, 'Economic Trends' (H M S O, July 1987).

Table 8: Northants Secondary Curriculum

CURRICULUM AREAS
*DESIGN, ENGLISH,
EXPRESSIVE ARTS,
FOREIGN LANGUAGES,
HUMANITIES, MATHS,
PHYSICAL EDUCATION,
SCIENCE, RE.
*AREAS OF EXPERIENCE

**PROCESS
FEATURES,** *eg.*
*ASSESSMENT
*RESIDENTIAL
EXPERIENCE
*WORK
EXPERIENCE
*COMMUNITY
INVOLVEMENT

THREADS
eg.
*COMMUNITY
EDUCATION
*EQUAL
OPPORTUNITIES
*ECONOMIC
AWARENESS
*ENVIRONMENTAL
EDUCATION
*TECHNOLOGY
*PERSONAL,
SOCIAL AND
HEALTH
EDUCATION

Notes

Chapter 1

1 John Maynard Keynes, *The General Theory of Employment, Interest and Money* (Macmillan, 1936).
2 F. A. Hayek, *The Road to Serfdom* (Routledge and Kegan Paul, 1944).
3 Geoffrey Howe *et al*, 'The Right Approach to the Economy' (Conservative and Unionist Party Central Office, 1977).
4 C. B. Cox and A. Dyson (eds), *The Black Papers on Education 1–3* (Davis-Poynter, 1971); C. B. Cox and R. Boyson (eds), *Black Paper 4* (Dent, 1975); C. B. Cox and R. Boyson, *Black Paper 1977* (Temple-Smith, The Adam Smith Institute, 1977).
5 'The Omega Report: Education Policy' (The Adam Smith Institute, 1984).
6 Cited in Cox and Dyson, *op. cit.*
7 Writing in Cox and Dyson, *op. cit.*
8 *Ibid.*
9 C. Burt, writing in Cox and Dyson, *op. cit.*
10 D. McLachlan, in Cox and Dyson, *op. cit.*
11 K. Gardner, *Crisis in the Classroom*, cited in Cox and Dyson, *op. cit.*
12 A. Flew, *The Pied Pipers of Education* (Social Affairs Unit, 1981).
13 C. Cox *et al*, 'Whose Schools? A Radical Manifesto' (The Hillgate Group, 1986) and 'The Reform of British Education from Principles to Practice' (The Hillgate Group, 1987).

Chapter 2

1 H. C. Dent, *The Education Act 1944* (University of London Press, 1966).
2 R. A. Butler, *The Art of the Possible* (Hamish Hamilton, 1971).
3 Third Reading of the Education Act (Hansard, 11 May 1944).
4 'Report of the Committee on Higher Education Appointed by the Prime Minister' (Robbins Report) (HMSO, 1963).
5 'Half Our Future – The Report of the Minister of Education's

Central Advisory Council' (Newsom Report) (HMSO, 1963).

6 'Children and Their Primary Schools – Report of the Central Advisory Council (England)' (Plowden Report) (HMSO, 1967).

7 Department of Education and Science, 'Education: A Framework for Expansion' (HMSO, 1972).

8 'Report of the Royal Commission known as the Schools Inquiry Commission' (Taunton Report) (HMSO, 1868).

9 H. C. Dent, *Change in English Education* (University of London Press, 1952).

10 R. Armfelt, 'Our Changing Schools: A Picture for Parents' (Central Office of Information, 1950).

11 *Ibid.*

12 *Ibid.*

13 Department of Education and Science, 'Circular 10/65: The Organization of Secondary Education' (HMSO, 1965).

14 C. Benn and B. Simon, *Half Way There* (Penguin, 1972).

Chapter 3

1 William Keegan, *Mrs Thatcher's Economic Experiment* (Penguin, 1985).

2 'Report by Her Majesty's Inspectors of Schools on LEA Provision for Education and the Quality of Response in Schools and Colleges in England 1986' (HMSO, 1987).

3 Audit Commission, 'Surplus Capacity in Secondary Schools: A Progress Report' (HMSO, 1988).

4 Geoffrey Howe *et al, op. cit.*

Chapter 4

1 'The Omega Report', *op. cit.*

2 'Special Educational Needs – Report of the Commission of Inquiry into the Education of Handicapped Children and Young People' (Warnock Report) (HMSO, 1978).

Chapter 5

1 'Further 555 girls to be offered non fee-paying places following High Court ruling in sex discrimination case' (Equal Opportunities Commission for Northern Ireland, Press Release 20 September 1988).

2 P. Barstow, 'When Fame is the Only Spur' (*Daily Telegraph*, 30 July 1988).

3 Howard Gardner, *Frames of Mind: The Theory of Multiple Intelligences* (Heinemann, 1984).

4 National Children's Bureau, 'Progress in Secondary Schools' (NCB, 1980).

5 See e.g. M. Rutter *et al*, *Fifteen Thousand Hours: Secondary Schools and Their Effects on Children* (Open Books, 1979).

6 Inner London Education Authority, 'The Junior School Project' (ILEA Research and Statistics Branch, 1987).

7 Inner London Education Authority, 'Equal Opportunities in the Curriculum in Single Sex Schools' (ILEA Research and Statistics Branch, 1985).

8 The Equal Opportunities Commission, 'Women Into Science and Engineering: A Survey' (EOC, 1988).

9 Home Affairs Subcommittee on Race Relations and Immigration, 'Bangladeshis in Britain' (HMSO, 1986).

10 Inner London Education Authority, 'Ethnic Background and Examination Results 1985 and 1986' (ILEA Research and Statistics Branch, 1987).

11 C. Burt, in Cox and Dyson, *op. cit.*

12 Stephen Jay Gould, *The Mismeasure of Man* (W. W. Norton, 1981).

13 Personal conversation between the author and Professor Goldstein.

14 L. S. Hearnshaw, *Burt: Psychologist* (Hodder and Stoughton, 1979).

15 See e.g. M. T. Taylor and G. D. Mardle, 'Pupils' Attitudes Towards Gender Roles' (*Educational Research*, Vol. 26, No. 3, November 1986).

16 R. King, 'Sex and Social Class Inequalities in Education: A Re-examination' (*British Journal of Sociology of Education*, Vol. 8, No. 3, 1987).

17 'West Indian Children in Schools – Interim Report of the Committee of Inquiry into the Education of Children from Minority Ethnic Groups' (Rampton Report) (HMSO, 1981).

18 Stephen Jay Gould, *op. cit.*

Chapter 6

1 C. St John Brooks, 'A Question of Merit' (*New Society*, 7 February 1985).

2 L. S. Hearnshaw, *op. cit.*

3 *Ibid.*

4 'Report by Her Majesty's Inspectors', *op. cit.* (1987). See also Bryan Rodgers, 'The Trend of Reading Standards Re-assessed' (*Educational Research*, November 1984), in which a close analysis of reading standards this century finds 'little justification' for claims of a decline in literacy.

5 'Survey by Her Majesty's Inspectors – Primary Education in England' (HMSO, 1978).
6 M. Galton *et al*, *Inside the Primary Classroom* (Routledge and Kegan Paul, 1980).
7 Alan Weeks, *Comprehensive Schools* (Methuen, 1986).
8 A. McPherson and J. D. Williams, 'Equalisation and Improvement' (*Sociology*, November 1987).
9 'Survey by Her Majesty's Inspectors – Aspects of Secondary Education in England' (HMSO, 1979).
10 'Report by Her Majesty's Inspectors on Educational Provision by the Inner London Education Authority' (HMSO, 1980).
11 Martyn Denscombe, 'Control, Controversy and the Comprehensive School', in S. J. Ball (ed.), *Comprehensive Schooling: A Reader* (Falmer, 1984).

Chapter 7
1 Inner London Education Authority, *op. cit.*
2 Department of Education and Science, 'Better Schools: A White Paper' (HMSO, 1985).
3 R. Pedley, *One Comprehensive School* (Penguin, 1969).
4 John White, 'The End of the Compulsory Curriculum' (*Studies in Education* 2, University of London, 1975).

Chapter 8
1 'Report of the Royal Commission on Technical Instruction' (Samuelson Report) (1882–4).

Chapter 9
1 Michael Heseltine, *Where There's a Will* (Hutchinson, 1987).

Chapter 11
1 Department of Education and Science White Paper, 'Education: A Framework for Expansion' (HMSO, 1972).
2 Albert Osborn and Janet Milbank, *Effects of Early Education: A Report from the Child Health and Education Study of Children in Britain Born 5–11 April, 1970* (Oxford University Press, 1987).
3 Jane Walmsley and Jonathan Margolis, *Hothouse People* (Pan, 1987).
4 Inner London Education Authority, *op. cit.*

Index